CU00656180

MADE LUCK

The Modern Musicians Field Manual

David Airaudi

3QP
First Edition Three Quarter Press, January 2019
00391576
ISBN 978-0-578-45986-8

Book & Packaging Design by Mike Hesse
Edited by Kathryn Huck

Los Angeles, California, United States of America

la famiglia

CONTENTS

PRE-PREFACE

This was never meant to be a book.

It was supposed to be just a rant after one meeting with a bunch of executives who were so ill informed, out of touch, and arrogant it physically angered me—not about the music or the business, but about the actual human beings who make the art.

This book was never meant to be published.

In the end what I had put down on paper sounded mostly like common sense to me; it overlaid with some common decency and a bit of insider info, but nothing most folks in and around music didn't know, right? But then I got a call. From a dad. His story was so cliché I don't even need to really go into detail other than his beautiful young daughter with a sultry voice posting on social media gets a message that says they can make her a star.

They can *make* her a star.

And I found myself getting angry again. I thought this shit was dead. Not the industry egos, but the near criminal public displays thereof. Imma leave the old powerful label guy sliding into a teenage girl's DMs for another rant and just focus on the fact that *they* don't *make* shit.

There is only one person in the universe who can make you a star— do you know who that is?

You.

To the music industry snake oil salesmen still out there peddling super stardom?

Fuck you.

Besides, stardom is not success, it's just a potential byproduct of a lot of hard work, self-doubt, made luck... Ok, ok, let me stop, I'm starting to rant and we're not even at the preface.

PREFACE

The music industry folks used to get it. I mean really get it. The business of it. The business people. They used to own it. They used to print money and shred that money for the raw green pulp with which to make more money. Heirloom money. And the music was phenomenal. This is not a sentimental jukebox book where I drop obvious classic song titles and purposefully obscure band names in order to prove my indie credibility and simultaneously conjure up glorious youthful memories that give you a warm and fuzzy glow, and thus subconsciously lead you to believe that this book is better than it actually is (it's not that great, trust me, I wrote it).

I mean shit, that used to be me. Label guy. Working weekends on 40 million dollar advance deals cuz some producer wants a new (rather large) house. 130 million dollar buy-outs for pop bands that popped twice. Doubling down on some icon whose posthumous songs are driving millions of dollars straight to the company bottom line while their estate is asleep at the wheel. A hundred people would work tirelessly across the globe to help an artist to "break," only to be told to fuck off at their first taste of success. And it worked both ways: an artist would work tirelessly around the globe only to be told to fuck off at the first sign their record is not gonna "break."

We love you, we need you.
We loved you, but now we don't need you.

Narcissism, mistrust, ambition, hustle, fights, smarts, creative genius and $100,000,000 of EBITDA. In a bad year. Old me. Analyst me. Belly of the beast me. Quiet in the back of the room me, before the war, before the mutiny. Before servicing stars and getting served subpoenas. Before the scars and hurt feelings. When friends were true and idols weren't assholes. When business was theory and spreadsheets king. Nobu, Leo, playmates, and expense accounts.

Now I can sit here and recount it all. I am certain it would be fun, I could rattle off a bunch of the big names I work/ed with to make myself sound mad important, but we are not here for my ego and your entertainment—we are here for your ego and my entertainment—more specifically how you, genius artist reader, get to make a living making noise that regular people like me will someday find entertaining. Besides, the reason I am in these rooms and get invited back to these rooms is cuz I figured out the golden rule early: keep your fucking mouth shut when no one wants to hear you speak. And that is 99.9 percent of time when you are a MBA kid in a room full of greats talking music, money, and genius.

Now before we begin let us delve briefly into why I even feel like I can speak on such matters.

One of the youngest execs at Interscope Geffen A&M Records, I quit with a crew of artist kids that I was told was so bad they wouldn't even be given the luxury of an opportunity to fail and they ended up ushering in a new era of music. I signed bands on promises that I failed to deliver. I pressed vinyl in Prague on Japanese presses and sold them by hand in Stockholm basements. I co-wrote songs, produced albums, dropped an artist friend off at rehab, drank smoothies on the beach with one of music's greatest and helped 250 kids spray the totality of a Berlin bar's beer inventory in each other's smiling faces. I bailed an artist out jail and then his lawyer tried to extort me. I hugged an artist after a show with only 10 fans, took a bow at Wembley, had an icon stand on a hotel table and rap me his album and another hide behind my couch after dinner. I got on the A train with brown bag full of $50,000 cash (just kidding IRS, this one is not true, I swear) and scrounged change from an artist moms' minivan floor to pay bridge toll. I have been hired by a mogul, fired by a henchman, knifed by a coward, ignored by a crowd, cried in the shower and snuck out the back of the famed Nobu restaurant. I held back tears on a 3-way phone call with the suicide prevention center and let them flow when I heard the song my friend wrote about that night.

This is how you truly learn the business. Up from the couch, the desk, off your phone and into the muddy trench that gets gassed by critics and raided by groupies. Where you wake up soaked and exhausted and deaf and then your trench mate lights your cigarette and you smile and smoke even though you don't even smoke and await the tour manager to berate you, justifiably, for being twenty minutes late to the lobby. Where you lose friends and find salvation in anything that changes the mood from heroin to hot yoga. Where money blows like mustard gas ethereally past your view of heaven. Don't reach. In fact, fuck your money. Just focus on selfcare and survival. Understand depression, anxiety, and doubt are prerequisites on this journey and the pot of gold awaits only those who finish. But this is not a therapy session and it's not a memoir so let's just say I have been on all sides of the circle (ok, ok my editor says a circle has no sides, but I say a circle has 2 sides as it is a line and is infinitely long so I'm just sayin' I have seen a lot and it all cycles and it goes on forever and if "all sides of the circle" is not an expression it should be and it is now so feel free to use.) So I have been on all sides of the circle doing all sorts of unmentionables from the classroom to the boardroom to the greenroom to the A-room and now I am gonna make an attempt to put some semblance of meaning around this business.

But this isn't business school—there are no shortcuts, no secrets, no handshakes, no illuminati code. This book is a ditch-digger's guide to the universe my friends, but you are in luck, cuz if you chose to be an artist, you are waist deep in a heap of shit.

All good, that's where the flowers grow.

P.S. Let me reiterate one thing before we begin. This book is for artists—those off-kilter art-pouring vessels who are just smart-crazy-brave enough to believe they can be successful in harnessing one's sonic soul and exchanging it for worthless green paper. Noble as fuck. Those simply seeking the paper can cheat off someone else's.

And yes, it is true that there is a non-art based approach to the art side to this business—we call these "science projects" wherein a global team of writers, producers, marketers, branding gurus, social media manipulators, algorithm whizkids, stand ins, pitch modulators, and someone willing to spend bags on bags of green paper get together to manufacture and sell audio arrangements that the data they researched says will be pleasurable to human earholes.

This is not that book.

If this book is anything it's a baton pass. It's cheat codes. The rationale for choosing an irrational life. A surgical handbook for those who have found themselves in an empty room with their insides hanging out.

Lets hang out.

I. THE NEW BASICS

ONE

Lesson one: The music business does not make music.

You make music.

The music business buys, sells, and licenses copyrights and hires the makers of said copyrights, a.k.a. you, the artist, on an ad hoc basis to market products and services related to these copyrights.

Yeah, that's correct, you are not even the most important thing at your own show. You know what the most valuable thing at a festival is? The beverage contract. Not all the artists, not the headliner, not you, the drinks. A magazine used to use your face to sell ads (now it uses interns to pretend it's still solvent a.k.a., not bankrupt a.k.a., it's bankrupt) and the festival uses it to sell lavender infused tap water.

You are trying to figure out how to get an extra all-access festival pass for your weed guy while the business is trying to figure out how the RFID chips they put in your wristband can someday activate a holographic artist your fans will subscribe to, pay for by cryptocurrency, and thus allow them to eliminate the need to spend their days figuring out how to get an extra all-access festival pass for your weed guy i.e., how to eliminate the need for you i.e., the artist.

Welcome the commercialization of you and your art.

Let's not get it twisted my friends, this is a commercial fucking endeavor. Yes, even for you "real" artists out there, sorry, as soon as

14

you put the tip jar in front of you, you are in the music business. If you truly don't want to be in the business, then you need to relegate your playing to acoustic sets in your Aunt Susie's backyard at family functions on the Sundays you can get someone to cover your shift at (enter big box store name here) and don't be insulted when your cousin Frank doesn't pay attention. That's art.

This is not an art book.

There is no art in letting musicians starve while we fight for scraps from technology companies. There is no art in losing an average of a billion dollars a year as an industry for a decade. There is no art in dedicating more effort on the VIP craft cocktail garden than the performers on stage. There is no art in market share. Cuz that's what we are doing as an industry; we used to advance artists cash to make art based on the projected future value of their earnings, i.e., the money they were gonna make from that art, but now we are leveraging catalog libraries of old artists old work to get advances for multinational conglomerate parent companies. And today we are basing our new "music" decisions on pop-up food truck sales, click rate, follower count and customer acquisition models.

We in this business pay lip service to progress, but are still using twentieth-century technology to calculate nineteenth-century copyright law applied to first millennial oration practices and then report it via management teams, most whom don't even understand this sentence. And that's not a knock, I got a MBA and a biology degree which makes me about as equipped historically to manage a band as a lightly avacadoed slice of hemp-quinoa toast, but shit has changed, even the toast.

This is not just true for music, it's the entire media landscape; we hit ludicrous speed sometime around the failed Armageddon that was Y2K (not to be confused with B2K) and hereafter we live in a tangled world where the background music in a meme can be of greater importance then a top 10 hit. And only maybe half the folks running this biz even know what a meme is. The other half are too busy trying to recreate the "top 10" hit definition by cobbling together a meaningless amalgamation of nascent media statistics (clicks) and hundred-year-old airplay metrics (radio). For what?

Did you know we as an industry still talk about revenue as "album equivalents"? We literally do a backwards calculation to change streams, downloads, etc. into albums. That's the same as if Apple measured its revenue in terms of "electric typewriter equivalents". Can you imagine the earnings call?

Analyst: Um, yes, Apple, how was revenue in Q2?
Apple: Great, we did about as well as selling 150,000,000 electric typewriters.
Analyst: Is that Good?
Apple: We're top 10.

Look, today the business of music extends way beyond just the music and thus a broad-based understanding of media, technology, brand, and consumer products is critical to nonlethal navigation thereof, but few get that and even fewer even get music and artists' role within it.

But it's all good. I mean it's not all good, but it's all good. I mean fuck someone had to lug those player pianos around and sell them door to door so artists could keep cranking out the ragtime. You think Scott Joplin loved the home furnishings sector? But it kept him in knickers and felt hats. Jazz hands!

And that's why we are here.

Wait, a quick, but critical caveat. Before you even get the luxury of participating in this music business madness you have to make mad music that matters. Music that moves. And that, my friends I will not teach you in this book. I can't. No book can so be wary of books, people, and/or classes that say they can.

What I can do is aid in the modern necessity of coupling your masterful sonic emissions with world-class business practice.

Ok, ok, lets slow down for a second–feels like we shot outta this cannon rather quickly and I don't want us to get ahead of ourselves. BTW, am I still making any sense? My mind feels like its full of cartoon thought bubbles popping up erratically in an empty room. Or that could be all the second-hand smoke on this this eight-wheeled bouncy house of a tour bus we have been calling home for the last month. Or perhaps fueling my digestive system exclusively with items designed to withstand nuclear fallout on a gas station shelf and causing 100% of my sleep to be liquid induced is not the best way to keep a clear head. Or maybe, maybe this cocktail is exactly what one needs to start to understand the music business. Maybe this is the secret industry recipe—a steady diet of fear, magic, asphalt, practice, angels, sweat, silence, anxiety, hallucinations, car service, models, champagne, hotel, motel, futon, floor, high fives, breath failure, stale weed, and bad pizza.

Maybe you need to get on the bus to get it. Maybe it's the act of stepping in and out of this madness, the navigating of the surreal dream world of screaming fans lined for blocks and the normalcy of a grocery store checkout counter. Maybe it is getting your every whim catered to for weeks, then still being able to make your rent payment on time. Maybe it's spending the money you make touring the world on doctor's visits for chronic depression while listening to everyone tell you how "lucky" you are.

Maybe it takes living in the dream to realize the dream does not exist. That a dream realized is by definition its death. Or maybe that's just some deep Zen shit I am projecting to rationalize my leaving my wife and kids at home while I rocket all over the world to stand next to the people other people want to stand next to.

I don't know. All I do know is that if you take this path seriously you will find out the hard way. And I know this for a fact as right now in this precise moment I would pay four hundred American dollars for a fresh salad and glass of water. A thousand for my own bed. But not today. We have a show in Rotterdam in five hours and we are six hours out. Shit. Where was I?

THE ~~MUSIC~~ BUSINESS

There is no such thing as the music business. There is just business. The "music" part was put on there to make you believe it is different, nuanced, some magical form of commerce that's somehow detached form the laws of physics. So men with high paying jobs could keep the jobs male and high paying. Business people can't come in, this is music! Music people can't come in, this is business! Women can't come in, this is, uh, why haven't women been able to come in again? Fiefdoms built on the backs of kids' art projects by telling those same kids told they couldn't possibly "get it."

Short chapter, important lesson.

Lesson two: Business is business.

Let's get it.

THE STUDIO

We begin our journey in the studio as it is where you will begin yours. It is literally the room in which you will transition from music as art-hobby to music as business. Now when I say "studio" here I mean professional studio. Not your bedroom laptop yelling at your little sister to be quiet studio, I mean a specified room soundproofed and financed specifically to capture audio waves with the intent of people not in said room to listen to said waves not for free.

If you have found your way into one of these rooms, you are on your way. If you have not, you are on your way to being on your way. Either way, your way leads through the studio. Anyway.

Now originally I wrote this chapter to walk you through the typical studio experience, but after a few drafts I realized that there is really not a "typical" experience and found myself getting into too much detail on the artistic side of the business so I edited it *WAY* down to just include some high level context to help you orient you in those early days of professional transition.

Lets begin.

Upon arrival to any quality studio you will find a buzzer door. State the artist name on the manifest correctly and gain entry. Continue past the non-functioning metal detectors; past the table with stacks of obligatory untouched music publications and tiny Buddha head; past the wholesalers assortment of teas guarded by sticky plastic bears full of honey that someday will be empty and made into bongs; past seven stacked cases of warm sugar-free Red Bull and into a red hued room with carpeted walls and enough tiny lights and knobs and deadened sound to make NASA jealous.

In the original draft, I went on to describe the common equipment and functions you find herein, but these are artists tools so I will leave that for you to discover/experience/master. I do want to leave in some practical advice, namely, do not be intimidated by the room, but don't start feeling yourself either. Wimbledon courts doesn't scare Serena, but she also doesn't dominate the sport due to the quality of the grass manicure. And these social media photos of artists with their hands in prayer position on the giant soundboards? Don't be fooled; they don't even know how to use that shit. As you'll learn, the folks who do don't take photos cuz they are too busy in the back changing the physical tape reels or smoking physical cigarettes, or both, simultaneously. In the beginning you just use the big soundboard for playback, i.e., playing music through the room's main speakers so you can hear the cleanest possible resolution of what you are recording, i.e., the main reason you are in the studio in the first place.

I wrote a bit about personnel you find in the room too, but for our purposes will just note a few key folks: engineers (people who get the sound from your body to a recorded format), assistant engineers (people who know how all the wires and nobs work), runners (people who go get you food and rolling papers) and industry douchebags (the non-artists who come in and act like *they* are at work). Which brought us to lesson three.

Lesson three: The studio is your workplace.

The studio for you is like church to a priest. All sorts of people will come in to catch a vibe, holler at God, and dip just in time to let everyone know they went, but for you, you have to stick around and attempt miracles. Hallowed ground. Or as close to it as most of us will ever get. But keep your head about you; deadened electrical hums are known to heighten the subcortex so it all can feel like a religious experience, like it's all happening in a low orbital space station lounge, but that will pass and soon turn mellowly euphoric.

Divine.

But the studio is no Sunday morning stop on your journey—the studio is your basecamp. And as any good adventurer knows basecamps are not on the ground, they are three quarters of way up the mountain. They are where you get ready for the summit with the gear and the team and the butterflies and the hope. Where you smile cuz it feels like an accomplishment, and it is, until you look around say "uhhh, shit" realizing the final miles to glory go straight up.

Dizzying.

Your studio basecamp might be a built-out basement, a retrofitted the hull of 1950s' schooner or the place such-and-such-a-band recorded such-and-such-a-hit in nineteen-seventy-such-and-such, but it just needs to capture dynamic frequencies in the manner in which you intended to make them. So don't be afraid of or rejoice in the big room, but also don't pretend you don't need it. A sawmill maximizes tree input for lumber output. A studio maximizes noise input for song output. You can woodshed all you want to but eventually you need to get into a room designed specifically to optimize your specific style of production and output.

Look, Jordan didn't spend his days shooting free-throws in his backyard even though he was perfectly aware he had a regulation size hoop there.

And sorry tech companies, don't believe your own marketing—studios are not going away, they are just evolving. And no, the pristine converted warehouse with the coffee bar you just built to make "content" is not gonna replace 'em either. Music making is not about content yield efficiency or cost reduction, sometimes the difference between an idea and a hit is a two-hundred-dollar tropical fern and three bottles of sparkling rosé. True story.

This is not a knock on tech company content farms or a reason not to shoot free-throws for fun at the park, you gotta appreciate all parties and all ways that might seek help aid you in your (to keep our previous analogy going) preparation for a perilous trek to new heights. But this is life and death for you. This is liberating mountain vista vs. soul crushing 9 to 5. No non-artist is gonna get that, or care, but you need to. So when rallying the squad and training you don't put your faith in an app, software, a corporate marketing department, your old friend from junior high with the Macbook Pro. Sure, maybe they all wear beards and beanies these days, but they are not Sherpas. And your sole focus, as you make the leap from art as hobby to art as business, is to get to the summit, alive.

Let's leave it here, you got music to make.

THE ~~MUSIC~~ BUSINESS DEFINED

When someone says "music" business they typically mean the "record" business and when they mean record business they typically mean something akin to the mafia. Dudes in suits strong arming deals, embezzling cash and shaking down poor dreamers to sell songs. Money on drugs on boys on boys on girls on lust on violence off rules. Rinse, repeat. The music industry is consistently depicted as a happy blend of total debauchery and organized crime. Maybe that's how the business was once. Maybe we are the only industry in history that Hollywood has accurately portrayed as-is, unable to embellish upon such perfect fancy. Some would have you believe this still. Anyone who tells you this version of what this business is is not in this business. Let's cross that fable off the list.

And I am not saying music is not a dirty business, it absolutely is. What I am saying is that that is not because it's unlike other businesses, but preciscly because it IS like other businesses. It is an attempt at monetization of products and/or services that are not biological necessities. But ours is a special kind of product and/or service as our product and/or service is actually a byproduct of the oft tortured soul of an eccentric genius who emotes sonically.

Done right, it is maddeningly entertaining. Done wrong its exploitative assholishness.

Lesson four: It's called entertainment for a reason.

The music industry is an arm of the entertainment industry. Any entertainment business that is not delighting your fancy is not good at its job and thus will not be a business very long. So yes, fanciful myths persist; in fact, they are perpetuated because the only entertainment businesses that survive are... wait for it... entertaining. So if you are a fan or just enjoying the show, all good, embrace whatever version of the music myth you want to, but if you are in this business and/or want to be in this business and/or are claiming to be aiding

24

this business you need to recognize that we are manufacturing entertainment. You need to understand the difference between the making-of and the marketing-of music and you need to be cognizant of the reality that surrounds the business operations of these two activities. I mean how many happy cows have you seen in the slaughterhouse yard? But roll into the grocery store and there they are, smiling bovine basking in the sun in the green grass meadow right there on the pre-packaged lump of pink flesh.

Smile for the cameras people.

Now, why the music business is held to task for not being forthright, altruistic with a healthy dose of humility is anyone's guess, I mean it is in the title—music *business* a.k.a. entertainment profit making a.k.a. amusement for cash. Did the guy who ran the Globe have Shakespeare's best interest at heart? Did Steve Jobs, RIP, have yours? But you love your iPhone and tear up when Romeo sips the slumber punch.

So, lets define:

The *entertainment business* is the commodification of fantasy.

The *record business* is the manufacturing and sale of chronicled music.

The *music business* is the monetization of harmonic sound.

That's us. So lets continue our definitions and define the scope of the "harmonic sound monetization" that we will explore herein:

By *business,* I mean quantifiable, value accretive, sustainable cash generating activities.

By *music,* I mean creative output of the audible variety.

So when we talk about *it*, the "music business," we are really talking about a *business* that uses audio output for cash profit. This seems simple to the point of silly, but its critical. We in this business talk of record streams and show guarantees, but those are just specific mechanisms by which one may choose to make money from audio. They do not define the business nor are they any more legitimate than any other.

So *it is* fairly simple right? The business? Well, it was. There was a system.

Old System: Record the audio, catalog it, register it as an intellectual property ("IP") asset that can be legally bought and sold, manufacture that IP on physical goods, control the distribution thereof, leverage the name, likeness and eventual celebrity of the creators behind the IP to go out and promote that physical good and take a fee from those activities.

The digitization of music puts a snag in that plan, but at its core it functions the same.

Herein is the bigger snag:

26

The problem with *it*, the music business, is that it is still functioning in that model. Funny to put it that way, but true. The continuation of our core asset-based income source (a.k.a. records a.k.a. songs) despite the fact that recorded music revenues have had a hall-of-fame-level collapse allows many business folks to call our last decade and a half a "correction" and deny the fundamental destruction of the old system. And now that streaming revenue is flooding back into the major label coffers it allows all the record business folks to call the "correction" "corrected" and go on denying the fundamental destruction of the old system. But streaming revenue is not up due to resilience of the traditional model nor strategic adaptations in the wake of the digital shift, in fact it is the opposite. As the industry sued kids and moms (Google "RIAA sues 12 year old") tech companies took the lead to build new music consumption models. The new-found revenue is due to Silicon Valley's thirst for data, subscriber acquisitions, and the continuing obsolescence of physical playback devices, all of which are funded by tech profits and private equity funds.

Labels are in the music industry the same way OPEC is in the auto industry–sucking the marrow out of dinosaurs while Dylan's grandson goes electric.

And I don't know why we let the live music folks continue to pretend that their revenue increases are not simply a byproduct of this same situation, i.e., the value people place on physical products has plummeted, while the value of experiences has sky-rocketed, thus consumers free cash has shifted from product (albums) to experience (shows). All of which is driven by advances in tech, and not just from streaming services replacing CDs, but from tangential services like social media dramatically increasing the benefits of experiences (assuming you believe in the new social currency of likes and favorites which, apparently, we humans, really, really do).

But the traditional system is fucking over people.

Geriatric rockers and their catalog maybe buoying the old guard, but I can assure you any kid growing up in an age of self-driving cars is not going to turn on a car radio on the off chance there is a sound they like spontaneously playing and deem that "entertainment". Nor in the age of VR (virtual reality) are kids going to pay eight hundred dollars to sleep in a dirty ass tent in some middle of fucking nowhere music festival campground to see an artist that any day now will be beamed into their living room while they live chat with ten friends. I mean there are holograms with social media accounts playing pre-recorded music on physical stages right now, how long are people going to keep up the ruse that our old business model is gonna sustain us?

Those in this, the modern business of music, need to come to terms with the fact that while a lot of horses were still bought and sold after the Model A, it doesn't mean that transportation based business model wasn't dead. You don't close up shop the next day, but you don't block new freeway construction and rejoice on falling hay prices. It is up to us to recreate a system by which we sustain the business that surrounds audio output so that artists can sustain themselves. Cuz at the end of the day, people still want the music. And the music is still what drives the business.

Lets get down to first principles.

The business of music is simply cash from sound, but shit is complex.

SHIT IS COMPLEX

So in everyone's defense, and I think I speak for everyone in the business when I say, my dude, this shit is mad complex.

Not the music business itself, as defined that's fairly straightforward, but it is the world that has become mad complex. There is just far too much competition for our senses these days and whether you are buying a winged full body speedo and diving off mountain tops or walking down the street watching video clips of people in winged full body speedos diving off mountain tops on a six-inch screen, let's just say the entertainment paradigm has shifted.

Today it's all about stimuli.

Stimuli served up via overlapping media formats and platforms creating an exponentially diverse array of attention grabbing tidbits, building subgenres upon microgenres of pleasure focused morsels, resulting in far too many variations of distraction, celebrity, idolization and cool for even the most digitally insatiable kids to get his head around, let alone some old music promotions head or music school professor to reliably decode, understand, and professionally manage.

Why am I speaking so broadly on the digital media age? Because the powers that be refuse to admit that we are no longer releasing music product in a media vacuum to a public that values ownership of our media product. We are no longer putting on shows in awesomely shitty stinky clubs to super fans. We are no longer screen-printing bland band names on scratchy tees and charging 10 times more than a department store tee. We can no longer simply demand an intrinsic value of music simply because we, a fraction of humanity, deem it "sacred." The truth is that that is just the subjective opinion of the niche cult called music nerds. Now I am a card-carrying member, but to expect the general populace to hold that same sanctimonious position on the basis that we think they should, is absurd. To use that as the founding principal of your business model is lunacy.

Music is just one stimulus in the sea of never-ending stimuli.

Even at the show, the festival, performers have been reduced to loss leader for farm-to-table popcorn, parking, booze and social media backdrops. An excuse to buy a new outfit and old drugs. Scoff you may, but next time you are noshing sushi from a pop-up food truck with 40-somethings on ecstasy in what was the weekend prior the middle of nowhere, check to see if that (or any other) major festival had to even announce their line up in order to sell out. Will give you a hint: They didn't.

And streaming services? Their product is not music, their product is the users a.k.a., the fans a.k.a., the people *you* bring to their service.

Look, the streaming music distribution firms have accumulated a few hundred million users, rake in a billion dollars every year only to lose money and beg at the altar of the capital markets so they are not forced to declare bankruptcy. The fact is these streaming "music" businesses are propped up by banks hoping your music will give them an advantage in selling people shit other than music. Which leads us to another obvious secret:

Big, square investment bankers don't debt finance music, they debt finance data.

This is where music is today: the stream of your song has more value as an indicator of your fans' purchasing habits than it does of their value of music. That Instagram post of you at the show (i.e., the real-time socially shareable evidence you are there) has more value than the show itself. The meme of a song has more value to a kid on a smartphone then the song itself. The people running the industry just got on (insert real-time socially shareable media platform here), are still trying to figure out what a meme is, and, by the time this book has been published memes will no longer matter. The ability and mechanisms by which we create, engage and share audio changes daily. This is not bad, this is not good, this just *is*. (Ohmmmm.)

The old timers are giving a proper disbelieving headshake, but these are facts. Queue the old timers shutting this book now. Sweet, see you at the Coachella vegan dim sum bar.

But let's stay here, because this is critical. Too many in our business take this as an affront to their love of music, to the career they have built, to how they have defined themselves in since high school, so I get not liking it or wanting to believe it, but this attitude is setting our industry back. Business people need to embrace that fact it is not an affront against music, it is the whole media world, the whole world that is evolving at record pace. (Pun intended, thanks mom.)

A silly lip-synching app for twelve year olds raises $100 million at a $500 million valuation and back to $0 in twenty months. Another one sells for a billion. True story.

Our business is caught in the middle of a battle to the death for people's attention. We didn't start the war, we didn't want the war, but we are in it and our precious music is being commodified and aggregated and exploited as attention fodder.

And what do we do? We double down on "breaking" acts.

Wtf does that even mean?

I mean, yes, I am aware (and will now make you aware) of the fundamental principle of music business physics that says: breaking an act = money. And true, when an act "breaks," it does generate a lot of revenue, but how exactly one "breaks" has never truly been defined. And those that say they know how are lying. That's because breaking an act is like irony, no one can define it, they just know it when they see it. And that is because it is different every time; every artist, every story, every style, every pop culture cycle, requires a unique set of circumstances, actions and doses of made luck. Even if you can pull it off more than once it's not cuz you get it, it's more than likely cuz you got great artists making great music at the right time; and you can just as easily quantify that trifecta as you can predict fruit cobbler deliciousness from a bee swarm.

But that doesn't stop us from trying to get records to "break" into the charts, artists to "break" into the industry, albums to "break" into the mainstream, but even though you did at one time "break" in music, you don't "break" anymore.

Not into music.

You do "break", but you break into culture. You break into media. You break into social networks and fashion shows and viral videos and gossip columns. You break into news feeds and episodic programing. You break into content, into advertising and modeling and directing and entrepreneurship. And before you break in, you break through. You break through the thick static blanket of fuzz that is layered over the daily lives of a voyeuristic citizenry obsessively looking for content and purpose and distraction and lust and leisure and escape. And belonging.

And to belong in the modern media ecosystem is to belong to a borderless world wherein music, art, fashion, film, books, theater, memes, photos, social commerce and the ten-second videos of you and your friends at dinner last night are fluid.

And if you think you do this by making music you don't.

And if you think you do this by making music you do.

(There is some Zen shit in this business-ish book, hold on to your green teas.)

You see, you do make music, but that music product gets immediately swallowed up in the aforementioned infinite stimulus sea. If that music is to withstand all the other stimuli assaulting us for our attention, it has to have a genuine impact on us. Your music has to have relevance beyond being a product (i.e., a song you can buy or stream), it has to affect our lives, jar us from our oversaturated media numbness. And that doesn't mean better marketing. It doesn't mean you have a line of perfume and a sex tape, it means your music has to matter to people. Really matter. And things that really matter in media become part of our culture. Whether for a moment or for a lifetime. And thus the business of "breaking" in music has become the business of leveraging music to matter in culture.

Great, so add another layer of complexity to an industry that has been hauling plastic discs and lighting rigs on flatbed trucks for fifty years.

And I know you, artists, hate the term "culture" as much as business folks hate the term "content," but get over it, they are not it, they are just terms mortals use to explain it. (More Zen.)

Look, you may not think of yourself as "culture," but I assure you the people that you are lending your name, likeness, ethos and music to do. The shoe company, the make-up company, the vodka biz, they are building their revenue, their brand and their credibility by tying themselves to you and your art. You are being booked to perform in an arena because you sell tickets. You are signed to that label because you sell music. You are in that magazine cuz you sell ads. You are on that blog so the maximum amount of people will click on it i.e., generate income. You move people.

This is not a bad thing; the bad thing is that we have yet to accept this and build our business accordingly.

In the modern music business your value as an artist is not in your ability to move product, it is in your ability to move people.

A song used to be something you sold, if you sold enough it had the ability to make you a star and a star had a career traveling around entertaining the masses. Now a song has the ability to put you in a position to potentially matter in culture. Whether you chose to act on that position and how you use it build a sustainable business (we will get into this) is up to you. Or perhaps the song is so fucking good your lack of action becomes your brand of cultural relevance, but even doing nothing is nuanced nowadays—you can be aloof, artsy, an IDGAF (I don't give a fuck) punk. But you can't escape culture, no matter what you do or don't do people are more than happy to put you in their preferred culture box and profit from the impact you are having on consumers.

Or as I told [deleted] (let's just call him a household name rapper): you move culture and culture moves markets so that means you move markets.

Again, this is not good, bad or otherwise, this is simply the evolution of music's consumption as part of the masses' media diet.

But wait, the cloud to the rescue!

Sorry, magically getting music from air is not a savior its radio. Radio was the old cloud. Magically getting music from air to your phone is the new cloud. Don't get caught up in the tech. Your iPhone stream is just a pocket player piano.

Now, importantly, because your music moves you into culture, you now have the ability to move ("break") from any of the various cultural microcosms. Smoky backwoods bar to national TV commercial to viral video to social media meme, you get in wherever and however you can.

And this is precisely why you cannot continue to rely on old methods of business and "breaking." You can't trust some old guy's gut or some antiquated industrial system when the scratchy sound on a grainy smartphone video loop posted to a social network as a personal joke has the ability to spawn a whole new genre of music. And you certainly cannot read a bunch of anecdotal accounts of what "great artists" did or do or didn't do to learn the business. You think they know better because they pressed a few knobs in a room that sometime later was deemed to have been better than average by some other guy who pressed knobs in some other room that was also deemed later to have been important? It's like a literary ponzi scheme of knob pressers. Like if I was the hose boy in charge of filling young Houdini's water tank now I can teach people how to get out of the straightjacket without drowning?

You know what great artists do?

They make fucking undeniably great music.

You know how?

Neither do they.

Probably by coupling massive amounts of talent and practice with a combination of misfiring neurons, a harrowing upbringing, and a healthy dose of narcissism that is filing a void society ripped from them early and unjustly. This is not a knock, these are time tested prerequisites of greatness (see future chapter entitled "Artists Are Not Made They Are Destroyed"). Don't believe me? Think of some greats and then think of their stories. Go on. Michael, Miles, Nina, Jimi, Dizzy, Cab, Django, Ledbelly, Dinah, Diana, James. Keep going. Show me a legend with a college degree and a picket fence who wasn't battling demons on the daily.

So I hate to drop the spoiler so early in my own book, but you want to make it in the music business? To know how to "break" into culture? You want the secret to success? To fame, fortune and ruin? (Eventually it all goes to ruin, see the future chapter I didn't write cuz it all went to ruin.)

Simple.

Make great music.

You want more specifics? Ok, you bought this book and/or stole it off the worldwide cyber highway, so I guess I owe you that. So here goes, if you want success in the music business, as an artist, please follow my patented, time-tested, industry-vetted, trademark registration pending, 3-Step Plan:

Write great music, record great music, play great music.

You want more fame, more money, more press, more followers?

Repeat.

Even more? Man you are greedy but OK, I will give you a sneak peek into my top secret 3-Step Plan 2.0 that is currently in beta-testing: Write music better, record music better, play music better. Repeat. You know why you are not getting anywhere in this business?

Because you are not following my 3-Step Plan. Because your music is not written, recorded and/or played well enough. "And/or" as you can't do just one, or two, it's a three-legged stool my friend. All cylinders must be firing on a sustained basis to break through the gargantuan clutter of a modern media ecosystem designed specifically to hog our attention.

Unfortunately there are no shortcuts to said plan. You cannot skip steps in this business. And while three steps does not seem like a lot, just wait till you try to take them. See I'm not saying it's easy, I'm saying it's simple. Lord knows I can't do it; I have a hard enough time on four-legged stools after a few drinks. Also why I am laying on a couch in a bus as I write this drinking a phenomenal amount of sparkling rosé. (See my future book, *Win Win: An Amateurs Guide to Starting a Booze Business*.) Yes there is marketing, yes there is money, yes there is payola and favors and movie trailer placements and free cocaine to strip club DJs, but there is no substitute for great music. Remember, this book is not about pop music "science projects", it's about career musicians operating in a merciless media ecosystem.

And is that it? Nope, of course not. You need a great team, drive, ambition, work ethic, made luck, radio promo, that sync license in that movie trailer, an opening gig, yeah, all of it, all I am saying is all of that shit is useless unless the music is AMAZING. The other shit might get a bad song on the radio, but it can't break bad music into culture. And once we get in then we gotta work even harder, hence the entire fucking book here, but let's not get the music part fucked up. Oh, and while we are here, lets clear up a few of our industry's classic clichés. The following reasons are NOT why you are finding it hard to break into the music business.

DEBUNKED REASONS AS TO WHY YOU ARE NOT "BREAKING"

You are not not breaking because people only like "pop shit." Pop means popular, you know who was pop music? Ellington. Sinatra. Simone. Gaye. Cobain. Beatles. Yeah, don't wanna be them. Listen, your lack of success is not because 99.9 percent of the people that listen to your music have bad taste (only 95% do, ha, kidding, sort of).

You are not not breaking because some executives and some snot nosed neighbor-of-the-chairman's kid who was promoted from intern to VP are sitting around a conference table somewhere plotting your demise. Those folks are working with what they got and what they got is a corporate job, Range Rover payments, alimony, entitlement, a good old USA bell curve work ethic, dry cleaning, a dozen other artists calling about the same thing you are, some fucking lemon cayenne maple juice cleanse for lunch that their partner is making them "do together" and your album. Which, was more than likely turned in late, over budget, with fifty people to work and twenty to "clear".

"Clearing" is the process of getting everyone who touches anything during a musical recoding project to sign legal paperwork, e.g. background singers, co-writers, studio musicians, producers, engineers, the guy who got the sandwiches. Some of these folks are union, some of them minors, some of them drug addicts with asshole lawyers, some of them Juilliard trained percussionist waiters with asshole lawyers etc., etc., etc. As it sounds, "clearing" an album is a massive, archaic pain in the ass and it must be done on ever record on every album ever. I did not write a chapter on it. But important for you to note that a LOT of painstaking boring-ass work goes on behind the scenes so that your music can be heard and you can be credited and compensated fairly. I know some good people trying to streamline this—they do gods work. Little g.

Oh and it's Friday, so the whole office is over everything, including your project, which has nothing to do with you, your music or sinister machinations; it's just the modern working persons totally understandable and justifiable lust for weekends that decimates all of the productivity of all businesses on all Fridays after 11 a.m.

Major labels, indie labels, agents, lawyers, the guy down the street pressing up posters as a favor for you, these people have lives that don't involve your dreams of success; their lives involve their own dreams of success. This is not shitty, it's genetics. I'm just saying the music business is staffed by humans. And while I love the evil genius, maniacal robotic destroyer of art and integrity image, if you've been inside the belly of the music industry beast you can see, while the talent therein runs the spectrum (as with every other human endeavor) there is for sure no one with the smarts and the stamina to sustain a calculated industry wide suppression of "good music."

Insert conspiracy theorists collective groan here, sorry y'all.

On the flip side, there is no one "good" enough to get people to like art that people don't like. So, where were we, yes, make great music. There is no room for not great. So while you are at it, go get great people to help with the transition we are in.

Wait, what transition?

THE HARBINGER PARADOX

Our entire industry has always been about the movement away from the center. The greatest music has always been made on the edges of society, of decency, of sonics, of technology; it has always been the outsiders pushing the boundaries forward, aided by bits of like-minded outcasts in what we called "scenes." And the centrists sit and criticize and reject; that is until they are ultimately proved wrong,

41

embrace these fringe ideas as their own and thus draw them towards the center. It has been the role of our industry from time immemorial to bring home what's discovered on the sonic frontier. And exploit it for money. Of course. You think Davey Crockett put those bear pelts up in a gallery exhibit? The guy made it to the U.S. Congress and starred in his own plays.

Let's pause for a music history lesson as told by a guy who knows very little about music history, me. Here are the only tentpoles you need to know:

1) The Big Bang
2) Sticks and rocks
3) The blues
4) The business of music

The move from 1 to 3 has little to do with this book (though never a bad thing to gain a bit of perspective, that essentially throughout the eternity of space-time the universe has done just fine without a music monetization apparatus), but let's take a shallow dive into the move from 3 to 4.

Post the advent of the blues and radio the twenty-first century music business went like this:

direct thievery

-

blatant lying

-

slight of hand

-

mafia

-

multinational corporations

-

corporate best practices

-

digitized thievery

-

tech based content

As I said, shallow dive, lots to clarify and expand on, but that's not for this book.

For this book let's talk about the current transition. This transition is not, as some would have you believe, and by some I mean nearly everyone who claims to "get it" in this business, a physical to digital transition. That transition already happened (in my profound music history treatise above we have already arrived at "tech-based content"). If you don't believe that and you work in music, quit and ask a teenager on your way home if they want a flash drive with 100 percent of your digital music library and see what happens. (The analogy works if I say 100 percent of your CD collection as well, but if you think a teenager cares about a CD you should have quit a long time ago.)

We are not in this current predicament because of a catastrophic shift in format that stripped the value out of music. It was no more a format coup than the move from sheet music to vinyl. Change is neither good nor bad, it is only our reaction to it that can be qualified as such. (More Zen shit, grasshopper.) Ok, so this is not a postmortem on medium nor am I Monday-morning quarterbacking 2 decades of the music industry's handling of the digital revolution, but let's just say the record labels probably handled it just about as well as any self respecting horse and buggy conglomerate circa 1908.

BTW, let's not assume that I am blaming labels and letting everyone else off the hook for stealing music for fifteen years and justifying said thievery by saying they support artists "other ways," like buying tickets and t-shirts. Bullshit. And it is true, people's entertainment dollars did shift away from recorded music purchases to festival tickets, headphones, sneakers, smartphones, etc., i.e., culture. But if a functional free copy of someone else's festival ticket was downloadable with one click on the Internet you would have stolen the ticket too. And the t-shirt and the beer and the hotel room and the car to get there. So stop. Just stop. You stole the music. Maybe you had to spend a few years dropping $18.99 on an album full of crap to get that one song you liked, but that still doesn't justify your theft any more then you pouring Pepsi outta your neighbor's bottle and justifying it because every time you buy a large soda at the corner store its 80 percent ice. If you don't want it, don't buy it. If you already bought it and don't like it, don't buy more.

See, I am working on this crazy theory on how to solve this issue of people trying to sell you shit you don't want. It's called Capitalism. I have not quite fully worked it out yet, but I have started by not buying men's yoga pants.

Ok, I am digressing.

But before we get back on track, I am certainly not letting the tech companies off the hook either. Everyone looking around at everyone else with chocolate on their lips standing on the shards of what is left of the music industry cookie jar going "what? who? me?" Look, if I didn't *personally* steal a truckload of TVs, but I built a pawn shop optimized for selling truckloads of stolen TVs, excuse me, items that fell off trucks, I am at fucking fault. These tech firms built businesses from stolen property. Allowing something you don't own commercially to make money for you commercially as a business model? That's not innovation that's called the mafia.

Oh wait, why is this starting to sound like it falls into my music history lesson?

I had better stop now before I run this metaphor full circle and end up saying that the whole music industry was built on commercialized theft of user-generated content i.e., music companies bringing mobile recording studios to the South where they collected "content", sold/distributed it to the living rooms in major cities by leveraging a technology artists did not fully understand, using a business model that gave artists pennies in return for ownership their music while corporations reaped 99 percent of the money selling discs and listening hardware. Yeah, I don't want to make that point—that might make some folks uncomfortable.

Ok, ok, just letting you know where your author stands on the last (hundred and) twenty years of our purported "transition."

Transitioning back to our true transition.

Today's transition is more formative then format. As we exit the age where corporations own 99 percent of the world's listened-to music and push post-Internet, we are evolving at an unprecedented clip. As noted, society itself is in this transition so it is not just music that speeds forward, but all of us, the centrist masses merging with the outlaw fringes. Areas that were once as different as the city and the frontier are starting to blend. No longer is it a treacherous life journey to find oddities, it's the click of a button. Goodbye regional scenes, hello global screens. You like it, you don't, you click it, you don't, you move on. And so it should be without surprise that an industry built on bringing home the latest sounds from the frontier would be in a tad bit of trouble.

Darwin called this The Harbinger Paradox.

No he didn't. Actually, I just made that up, but that sounded dope right? Like I was about to drop serious knowledge? Maybe I will just make it up now so people down the road can say, "You know Airaudi called that The Harbinger Paradox."

The Harbinger Paradox: The rate at which art travels inward from the fringes of a society to the centrist masses is directly proportional to the richness of overall culture. Thus that produced on/by the fringe must be increasingly novel and thereby will increase the richness and thus the rate inward. This acceleration will continue exponentially until a point of terminal velocity is reached at which there is simultaneous adoption of ideas at the fringe and center; wherein the fringe and center will collapse into themselves thus eliminating all culture.

While not quite to terminal velocity, we are on the lee side of increasingly fast-paced culture creation and adoption. And format is merely a variable therein. The Harbinger Paradox is challenging the underpinnings of what makes not just music, but art relevant in our society.

Our art, music, has been a core driver of culture for a hundred years and a predominate form of culturally significant media for fifteen hundred, but we are rapidly exiting the age wherein music, as a stand alone means of mass communication, is a dominate form of human interaction.

Music matters less.

Ok, not to you. Not to me. But the fact remains that in the aggregate global landscape of media product, music's intrinsic value is being reduced.

I believe it was Darwin who said, "It's evolution baby."

Or was it Bono?

Achtung.

~~ART OVER EVERYTHING!~~ A HARMONIOUS MIDDLE GROUND BETWEEN ART AND MOST EVERYTHING!

The line I loved when I got into this business was "music is different." Nope, sorry. The music business is not different in any other way then semiconductor business is different than the banana business is different than the investment banking business. That bit of thinking bit us in the ass to the tune of $50B of global revenues when digital-file-sharing came, and it will bite us in the ass again when AI arrives so we need to get things humming in the meantime.

And this is not your problem any more then veganism is not the ranchers' problem. You and your team can no longer hide behind "artistry" and must start being honest about the fact that the difficulties of making art into a business are only increasing and so there must be a cohesive effort on all fronts. True, undeniably amazing music, as with all art, will break through the infinite stimulus sea, but without a sustainably pioneering business architecture supporting a great plan well executed by an amazing team of passionate and skilled individuals working collectively and tirelessly towards a singular goals there will be no foundation on which to make and perpetuate undeniably amazing music.

Man, that sounds lame. True, but lame.

Btw, there are times when you can and should stand up and invoke the name of art, namely when you are producing a body of work that is so on point and so ahead of its time that no outsider can truly understand its brilliance until the art is released and stimulates the hearts of the masses. Note, all music needs to be ahead of the curve by at *least* a year if you hope to make any kind of impact in this business as it will take at *least* that amount of time to get it recorded, released and digested by the early adopters (the necessary trifecta to then have the masses glom on), that's not what I am saying here. I am saying that you can no longer use "art" as an excuse. You can't make avant-garde music that is not great and then claim that it's the suits that don't get it. Of course they don't, they are suits! And we just said you are at least a year early. So it's up to you to be honest with yourself. And when everyone around you is not hype or faking hype (you know damn well when they are) or worse when you are faking hype (you know damn well when you are) you need to be able to check yourself and go back to step 1 of our 3 steps, make better music. Remember, no one is gonna believe in you more then you, ever, so don't go around claiming the business is in your way (it most likely will be!), just make art that gives no fucks about the business.

This goes for the team too.

A large piece of today's art-business issue is a classic industry scenario—the team around the artist blaming everyone else for, well, everything that is not going well. That's the definition of a shit team. Look, no one gets it all right every time; if we are gonna ask the artist to be honest with themselves so must the business people. A shit team is in fact much more detrimental to moving the business forward then say, a shit label. A shit label blames the artist. At least it is expected from a label, that is a standard corporate CYA (cover your ass) excuse and it won't impact the label taking a hundred more shots at success with a hundred new acts. The artist team on the other hand is in a trusted position of power. Blaming business entities indiscriminately can derail not just an album project but the whole of an artist's career as continually pointing fingers outward allows you to justify your mediocre team and/or mediocre art. If your team preaches to you that you just make music and it is up to everyone in this business to make money they are incorrect.

Someone has to plate and serve the dinner, that's us lame business types, but we can't make people eat it and we sure as hell can't make people like it, best case we can convince them to bite.

Making money is your problem. It has always been your problem. It's just now front and center to your life as an artist. And this evolution may suck and be lots more work, as discussed, but it happened. You didn't have to worry about looking good in the 1970s because there was no music video, you didn't need to have the Internet on lock in the 1990s, you didn't have to be a master photo-filterer in the 2000s, but now somebody on the team better excel at the social media arts. And AI is coming to kill the social star. So as an artist today you have to be able to whip that music into an aphrodisiacal cocktail of noise, art, self obsession, eccentricity, humility with just enough voyeuristic indulgence to let the masses even give you a shot to break through the afore mentioned stimulus superabundance.

Ok then, first principles.

What we are really doing here, or you are really doing out there, is building a music catalogue, which you will then leverage to build a career in a world that no longer operates by some antiquated system wherein people pay gobs of money to own said music catalog (they may pay labels gobs, but the label pays you drips). And that is not a job for aloof artists surrounded by yes-men, it requires you to take charge of your life and your business.

You are the CEO of your company, like it or not. And you should. Cuz this does not mean you are a future mogul, doing your own branding deals and turning your back on the muse (maybe you are), it just means that you are in charge and responsible for a company whose product suite is derived from your soul.

Better you then, well, anyone else.

Plus it's kinda what you have been asking for the whole time right— ownership and control of your music? But if you get that then guess what? You are in charge of the business, too.

Is it a bit of a surprise actually, that this "holy grail" of ownership and control is now readily available, yet artists are still complaining as if it's still legend. But I get not doing it, doing it is hard and requires a broad base of expertise most artists don't have nor want to have— hence when the artist path presented itself it was chosen over, let's say, school or a day job. But before we blame artists for being, well, artists, let's take a look at why this business utopia is so evasive.

The obvious key hindrance to you taking this path is the simple lack of business support available outside of a "sell your songs for a loan" (a.k.a., a record deal—we will get into that soon) and play live until your body falls apart (a.k.a. tour—we will get into that right after).

And central to this void is our industry's insidious viewpoint that artists were somehow unworthy of such services. The word "kid" is thrown around a lot in the music business. And yes, some of these kids are kids, but that's not how they mean it. If you look at other industries, age is not a prerequisite for innovative product development. A 20-year-old suburban white hacker can raise $10mm on an idea, but a black kid from south LA somehow can't be trusted with $50k to make a product with real short term returns? This is a business book so I won't get into the other issues here, but let's note that they are noted.

And if one more venture capitalist tells me they "don't invest in 'hits' businesses" when their portfolio is software I'm am gonna punch them in the neck–yes I know it's code, but guess what, you are literally still betting on one kid on your roster sitting down and writing a hit.

But let's not go too hastily into the artist-need-to-be-business-people idea, that is not what I am saying.

A handful of people out there use the "artists should be CEO's" line, but these people don't understand the business either. You can't just be a great artist and decide to be a great CEO. It is no more a switch you can flip than any person sitting at any desk in the world can flip, you do not just walk into the boardroom one day cuz the muse visited you and you decided to run the show.

The fact is most great strategic commercial operators typically make lousy artists. In the same way most artists make lousy strategic commercial operators. So I am not saying you need to literally operate your business (that's the COO's job not the CEO's anyway), I am saying you need to think about it like a business. And I don't mean think as an actual business, I mean what I said, "*like*" a business. You are not drafting steering decks and blowing out five-year cash flow projections; you are the visionary, you are responsible to plot the path and draw the map for the rest of us to follow. And if you can get a squad of folks to do that work while you are on the art path, let's go.

Cuz great CEOs captain their ship; they don't steer, swab the deck, plan the route and troll off the back all at the same time. They do set the course, hire the hands and battle the big storms when needed to be sure we all arrive on time.

Your label is not working the record? You got the wrong label. Project not being executed efficiently? You got the wrong day to day. Revenue not optimized across all your activities? You got the wrong manager. Bad deals with bad rights? You got the wrong lawyer. You know whose fault that is? Yours. That's why when a tanker runs aground with a drunk skipper killing a bunch of cute sea creatures and pristine shoreline the CEO resigns. Were they the one knocking back peach schnapps surfing internet porn on top of a million barrels of crude? Of course not, but it's their fucking team, it's their fucking responsibility, it's their fucking company. You can blame whomever you want but that ain't getting the gallon of Quakerstate off that seal pup's face next to your logo off the Channel 4 News loop.

It's a rough gig I know. But the key here, the key piece that even these people who seem to understand the artist/entrepreneur theory don't seem to get is that you know what a great start-up CEO also knows?

When it makes sense for someone else to be the CEO!

And there will be a day when that comes, when you can pass the baton to a trusted colleague to do what they do best, run companies, while you do what you do best, make art. Someday you will be chairman of the board, but today, alone in your studio banging out beats, you are the CEO of your music business. And great CEOs don't need business cards and DIY bibles, they need vision, heart, and a middle finger strong enough to withstand all the faces you gotta stick it in.

Now the **best byproduct** of our industry teetering on oblivion is that it is tilting the table back in the artists' favor. An artist has never had this much control over the details of their career, from what kind of music they make, how they make it, who/where/how/when it comes out, even how much they charge. The result is a ton of fiercely nonconformist artists making arguably some of the best music in decades and releasing it the most innovative ways in history. They don't call themselves CEOs and they don't need to, but many of you sure act like it.

The **worst byproduct** is that a large swathe of our traditional infrastructure is being wiped out thus a lot of talented artists and music-loving workers are unable to make a living. Don't mistake my statements that it takes more than a love of music to make it in this business today for callousness against those that haven't been able to make it out the other side. It fucking sucks, these are my coworkers, friends, many of whom I have fought beside for years; I am just saying if you share the recent history of the music business with a Detroit autoworker they will give you a hug, but not shed you a tear.

The **scary byproduct** is that we are now rapidly populating our industry with more and more diametrically opposing brains. Corporate CEOs with bigger spreadsheets, more metrics, richer data sets and increased analytics. Artist CEOs with more creative ideas, less boundaries and an expanding vision for their own future.

Art vs. everything.

Now in tandem with our rapidly evolving data, skill sets, and best practice methodologies, we have also advanced into the age of musical ubiquity. Today anyone can use free software to make music and upload it to the world. Music has never been able to be created as simply and reach larger audiences faster. No talent required. But as the industry bemoans the resultant sea of mediocrity and noise they are missing both the rationale and the point. Music today is experiencing awe inspiring and unprecedented advancement.

Look, of course when you have a higher volume of musical attempts you are going to get a higher volume of terrible results. Ask Kobe, ask Curry—more shots equals more misses, but it also equals more makes, more show and more records broken. Add that to the fact that until recently you couldn't actually hear everyone's work-in-progress, so it may feel as if there is an exponential rise in amateurism, but really it is just exponential access to works-in-progress. And everyone sucks when they first start to do anything. Kobe and Curry didn't post video of them shooting hours and hours of free throws in high school. But guess what, to get great, they shot hours and hours and days and months and years of free throws in high school.

My point is that as more and more people pour into the creative process the whole medium is being challenged and this is good, this is progress, this is moving the bar higher and higher. It is as if Darwin was able to sneak in and sprinkle a little hot sauce in music's primordial soup. To compete at this sustained pace of music development as an artist you better evolve and adapt or get out of the gene pool. Everything is hyper-sped up now.

Kids are making feature films on their phones, starting multimillion-dollar businesses from their school cafeteria and doing double back flips on snowmobiles and what, the world's musical talent is just supposed to coast into the new millennia playing ragtime on a rented trombone?

So tell me again about the part where kids are missing out because they can't spend seven hours sifting through cardboard squares to spend the entirety of their newspaper route earnings guessing that there might be three to six minutes of auditory enjoyment whenever they have the time to sit alone in their room and spin a mechanical wheel with a needle on it that generates sounds? Hmmmm.

We lament kids posting "bad" music online and not playing instruments, but today, if you actually picked up a clarinet and learned to play because you heard a song you liked odds are that whole genre would have come and gone before you can squeak out Twinkle Twinkle. Post-oboe-horncore. And what, it's not a skill if you tap notes out on your phone, but it is on a metal pipe with holes? You think you just download an app and pop out hits? Besides it's all cyclical, instrumentation is coming back as I write this and could be gone by the time you read it. And I am all for instrumentation and musicianship—I only work with artists that have tactical music making talent—but it's like telling a carpenter they have to use adobe bricks: good house, bad skyscraper—whichever you prefer to live in is not good or bad, it's simply a matter of preference.

Personally I prefer Joshua Tree, but I am talking about business herein and there is no adobe in Midtown Manhattan.

Live and let live, people.

I believe it was again Darwin who said, and I am paraphrasing, "progress is a relentless motherfucker." Cuz progress requires change. Change requires work. And working towards unknown outcomes is scary. But that is where we are. Our art form, music, is now all wrapped up in all these other industries – technology, fashion, media, "lifestyle" – there's enough overlapping layers and inter-joined crevices to make a Venn Diagram blush. The only guarantee as to what will survive music's primordial pond is that it will not to look like something we are accustomed to.

Its gonna grow feet and make it higher ground. It has to. Survival is at stake.

So lets get practical shall we?

II. SAME OLD SONG

LABELS AND YOU

I got in a cab the other day en route to JFK with one of my bands, and the driver asks if we are "in a band or something?" The bass player says, "yes" and the cab driver immediately says, "Cool man, look out for those labels, they'll fuck you every time." Followed by a tale of "guys he knows" doing "big things" only to have it all squashed by "shady record labels."

Here we are, a crew of professional musicians, multiple albums into a major label relationship, heading home from playing a festival in Central Park and this fucking cab driver is giving us a lecture on the perils of the music business. It boggles my mind as to how some people think they know the ins and outs of running the music industry just because they like the product. I mean, imagine me telling that exact NYC cabbie how to better do his job; and not because I know how to drive, but because I enjoy watching people who drive for a living, drive. I wonder how long before I am tasting NYC blacktop.

The music business is only "shady" in that it is misunderstood. (Yes, specific people in the music business and/or their individual actions maybe shady, but that is the case within 100 percent of business and large groups of humans.) And I don't mean misunderstood by fans watching Hollywood documentaries and social media rants; there is a lack of understanding as to what the business is even for those in this business. Some of this is forgivable, temporarily, as most people get into music through a passion for sound as art not a strategic assessment of the underlying business model, but at some point you gotta dive into the boring business stuff if you want to survive.

Historically, labels have been the businesses that have been responsible for the production process of recorded music, which, until recently, has been the main money driver for the industry and the artist. They identify and sign talent, record music, market, promote, manufacture and distribute product; they make money from the sales and licensing thereof.

This much we all seem to get, but let's look closer.

Most people believe record labels make music; they don't. As noted, artists make music. Labels operate by turning music made by artists into commercial products. They drive revenue by taking these music products into the marketplace. They build value by amassing catalogs of intellectual property assets. Seems nuanced, but it explains a lot–like why artists are often treated as dispensable; within the label framework you are merely step one in turning raw material into product–you are lumberjacks, lab scientists, software engineers, and dare I say, artists–and thus your promotion and push to "stardom" are merely marketing tactics used to sell more products.

This is also why when Napster allowed for music to be traded for free, kids rejoiced, music employees tried to figure out how to use it to sell more records, and label owners sued the shit out of everybody. They weren't worried about music sharing, they were terrified of vaults of valueless intellectual property assets.

See you make music, but a label makes a catalog of copyrights.

The record label business model is an annuity model; they purchase

IP assets in the form of song copyrights whose long-term discount value is projected to be higher than the price paid to acquire and take to market. This model varies widely from the traditional consumer product model wherein goods are created, sold, used, and repurchased. Even though they were once in vinyl and CDs, labels' core business has never been in consumer goods.

This is where you come in. In order for labels to operate, legally, they must own the rights to the music, i.e., own the copyright, so they make contractual agreements with the makers of the music, i.e., the artists, to gain such ownership – that is called a record deal.

RECORD DEALS

A record deal is an intellectual property rights negotiation.

Oh man, I just fucked up every artist's year. How fucking lame is this? An intellectual property rights deal? Sorry, but that's what you are doing.

As noted, a record label is an owner and promoter of IP assets. This is important to remember as while you are parting with (potentially) music gestated in your very soul (hopefully) and ruminating upon what it means to be an artist, the label is running discounted cash flow models (optimistically) valued against future market based annuities (theoretically). I don't care how genius you are, how many fans you have, etc. etc., you don't "cool" your way to immunity from of underlying business principles involved in deals with multi-national conglomerates.

As for the cabbies and the know-it-alls, here is the obvious truth about record label / talent relationships:

If you are a talented young kid without a smart and savvy team of people around you and you take a large sum of money from a global corporation, you are gonna end up getting fucked. That's on you.

If you are a global corporation who gives a talented kid without a smart and savvy team of people around them a large sum of money, you are gonna end up getting fucked. That's on you.

Labels are not to blame. Artists are not to blame. Let's get to the crux.

THE CRUX 1.0: All record deals are bad deals.

All record deals are bad deals not because of they are evil, but because any deal that ends with a party thinking they lost is a bad deal. When you cut deals you want both parties thinking they won something and it ended fairly. When *both* parties think they lost? That is a horrendous deal.

And that is the typical record deal.

The physics of this is unsustainable. You begin with two parties with a historically adversarial mindset, stir in a bunch of high-stakes, high-emotion, high-stress work that requires high-cooperation add to it the fact with one of the parties possibly (definitely) high and then try to quantify the insanely subjective product that is sellable art.

Think about it, this is an artist's soul, their innermost thoughts, perhaps their life's work and now they are not even in the room. It's just two lawyers, one of whom is taking a commission off the gross income from deal the other with a random corporate job who is trying to get the lowest price and the least amount of oversight from that artist as possible. And both will have literally nothing to do with the project once they leave the room. ZERO. You made your opus and they are fighting over a half point royalty reduction in the case that physical versions of your to-be-created album get returned more than ninety days after a wholesaler bought it; assuming of course that wholesaler is still in business, you care about an album format and anyone bothers to notice this tiny line in the contract.

What super cool business did you think you were in again?

I once had a lawyer send me an email demanding an extra royalty point and mocking me because I wasn't prepared to provide a semi-annual accounting to his client. Exclamation points included. "Standard deal language" he said. Meanwhile my friend who was off his meds and using music as an excuse to stay alive had finally peeked his head out of his darkness with five songs he is proud of— we call it an EP to keep the positive trajectory of his life intact and yeah, we realize we its likely not gonna make a dime, but it will provide a billion percent increase in his self-confidence, wellbeing and safety. And here is some lawyer insulting me, holding up the release and thus literally play with the fucking mortality of my friend for a meaningless deal point. I am digressing, but fuck. We all gotta be reminded that this is a human being business sometimes (all the time).

Now here's where things get complicated.

Remember, these two opposingly-incentivized lawyers minds are duking it out on behalf the artist and the label–which are also of two opposing minds! This time it is creative v. quantitative. This rift is due to both minds being skilled in unrelated fields, having opposing definitions success and differing methods to achieve it, so honestly it is crazy that most deals even get done. And wait, that's not all, the creative v. quantitative rift is not only between the two parties' minds, a creative v. quantitative rift also exists *within* each of their minds!

Zen shit *and* neuroscience shit in this book, what are we doing?!? Wait, stay with me...

See, part of every executive wants to be associated with legendary creative works—not only will that generate more money, but it is the professional currency they will trade to grow their career (get a promotion, write a book). And every artist wants great executives in order to attain the highest level of compensation for their output, because they too have a career to build and who doesn't want/deserve to be fairly compensated for their work. It's a multilayered creative and quantitative Gordian Knot.

Unfortunately, the result is typically compromise and bitterness in the name of expediency and money.

So that's a record deal, but lets pause for record label basics.

THE BASICS

Record companies are the traditional financiers and sellers of music content. (Again, I am not a music historian and I am drinking copious amounts of sparkling rosé, so spare me the letters, this is the gist of things, I'm in the gist business.) We will get into some deals below but essentially, gist-wise, a label when they find an artist they believe is a ~~wise~~, ~~smart~~, ~~prudent~~, not-totally-insane investment, pays said artist an advance, this advance is meant to be a living stipend while that artist makes a series of records.

Now "records" aren't records in the record business; our "records" are your "songs" or "tracks," your "records" are our "albums," and the guy with the SXSW t-shirt tucked in to his Dockers playing foosball at the office calls it "culture-based content," fuck that guy.

Artists deliver the music, a set of records, a.k.a. an album, to the label along with the packaging art, lyrics, writers splits, credits and all relevant information as to who did what in the record making process from writing the songs to changing the tape reels. (Everything must be "cleared" remember?) The label readies that music for manufacturing via two processes called mixing* and mastering**, then manufactures, markets, and promotes those records, sells them to third party distributors and licenses them to anyone who wants to repurpose it for use in their commercial activity e.g. film, TV, games, retail space, etc. The label owns the music and pays the artist after enough money has come in that it covers, "recoups," their initial advance i.e., investment + expenses your lawyer hopefully didn't cave on i.e., never.

Mixing: all the individual sounds recorded on a record come in as individual tracks. Remember those giant mixing boards from the studio that no one know how to use anymore? Well, each of those rows of lights and knobs represents one track-like the guitar is one track, the vocal is one track, each drum—snare, tom, kick—are each on separate tracks. They don't turn them on anymore, but back in the day every one of those rows had a corresponding microphone picking up a singular sound. Computer programs do this now, but to the same end— clean tones that can then be manipulated, tweaked, and "mixed" in with all the other sounds. Most likely you capture multiple vocals, multiple guitars, tones, and layer and stack them all in and why not, no cost, just time and hard drive space. Once you have it all down you literally mix them, blending all of the tracks, all of the sounds on a record to get them to sound the way the artist wants them to. Mixing is an art, it really is, and I am no artist and I am in the self-described sparkling rosé fueled "gist business" so note there are lots of methods and a gazillion skillful nuances I am leaving out, but, again, that's the gist. All you need to take away from this is that it's a critical part of the business process.

Music without a mix is a salad without dressing.

**Mastering on the other hand is a total fucking mystery. I am con-vinced even mastering engineers, the cats that master, don't under-stand it. Basically, mastering takes those final, mixed records, adjusts some frequencies and levels them out making them sound the same and play at the same volume across all formats—CD, radio, new phone, shitty boombox, car, etc. The one thing I can say though is that you can distinctly feel the difference after a great engineer has done a* *great job mastering, but I still could not tell you why or even how you can tell, let alone how they do it. Mastering is New York pizza, when it's done right its incredible, when it's done wrong it's still not terrible, but how the fuck that guy in that little shop makes flour, water and tomatoes taste delicious in a way that is un-replicable out of the tri-state area is a Sphinx-onian riddle for the ages. Another critical part of the business process, don't skip mastering.*

These days even the mixing and mastering is often done before the records are turned in to the label; again, lots of ways to slice it, this is not a record making book, I am talking mixing and mastering only because most new artists don't realize how critical a component of the process they are. I will leave the record making to you; go get someone great to do it and let's move back to the business.

Or rather, let's get into what to expect as you move into the label business relationship arena.

But before you get to talk business basics you gotta get some attention, so let's take a step back and talk about how one arrives to the deal making table in the first place.

GO:

You start by working your ass off to build a fan base. If you don't know where to begin, revisit step 1 of my patented 3-Step Plan. You make some music, you get your social media outreach rolling, hustle up some shows (we will get into touring later) in an attempt to get enough people interacting, talking and sharing your music in hopes that it will yield a significant enough volume of data, metrics, numbers and water cooler chatter to get the label's attention.

Wait what? That's a shitty way to put it isn't it?

But it's true. The business of it. In the business of it, your being "discovered" is the convincing of a company to risk investing a lot money on you, an artsy kid with gargantuan dreams, likely little interest in traditional rules or societal norms, 50 percent chance of regular intoxicant misuse, 90 percent chance of childhood hardships, and 99 percent chance of taking 99 percent the credit and 1 percent of the blame. Now again, this is not derogatory, this is the recipe for successful artists; rule-following kids with realistic goals, a stable quality home life, a penchant for charitable giving, sobriety and humility don't often make legendary musicians. More likely they are busy making college loan underwriters very, very rich.

So you, artist, go drum up that interest. Not by thinking about it the way I just put it, but by just doing it; working tirelessly, harder than anyone thinks the human body can manage. Asleep at 4 a.m., up before noon; jumping on the internet, pushing your message; all-nighters in someone's extra bedroom they turned into a home "studio"; calling in favors to every person you have ever met with a creative skill to help with art, videos, fliers, photos, digital, messaging. Hustling shows, hustling producers, hustling food. Fighting off every distraction from parties to relationships to social media by making music for parties and relationships and social media. Ignoring all the doubters and sound-advice-givers, the relatives every holiday function asking when you are going to get a "real job" and that is if you are both lucky enough to have an operating family unit and can afford the trip home. Forgoing all the paychecks and Roth IRA contributions; trading mattresses for couches and counting victories by the number of kids in the crowd that know the words to your songs as you stick around to watch the headliner play the slot you dream of being yours. And it should be. And it will be, because you know in your heart that there is nothing else you should be doing, nothing else you could be doing; forget want, you *need* to do this like you *need* plants to blow grade-A oxygen into your lungs when you open the window of whoever's apartment it is this week at which you are lucky enough to be able to crash.

Whew.

Simply put, you are doing it. You are living the dream. And this is the only way to do it. Overnight success in the music business is the culmination of years upon years of eschewing every societal norm in relentless pursuit of an impossible fantasy. It is tens of thousands of songs strung like arrows plucked from the soul's quiver and aimed at anyone within earshot. It is the luck you make.

Now the fans are materializing i.e., the metrics look good i.e., the followers online are ticking up and up, comments and sharing is strong, song streams are registering and are included on some indie playlists, homemade blogs and/or college radio, show attendance is capping out in smaller rooms, press requests are hitting the inbox. All of a sudden it feels like the long hours of combing the psyche and working side jobs is starting to bear fruit i.e., yielding data sets defined actionable by risk averse corporations.

Isn't that why you got into this business? To someday have your music take you to a place where you too can be considered a low risk actionable data set?

Fuck yes, I am a low risk actionable data set motherfuckers!!!

(Note to self: Register, trademark, my new band name "The Actionable Datasets.")

Cue the wooing.

Label wooing comes in three forms: money, drugs, and promises. I know because I have offered all three. I know because I have taken all three. And you think about it, when they offer it, a record deal. You question it, you sleep on it, you smoke on it. You know you have built it all yourself to this point, they forced you to; they didn't believe in you—nobody did, which is understandable because these are business people with day jobs, not fairy fucking godmothers. (If this was the fairy godmother business you'd have glitter on your hands right now.) And you abstained from shortcuts here, you built your fan base outta hard work, resilience, and sleeplessness; you know your fans, you know they love you, and you know that you know better than anyone what your people want to hear and how to make and deliver that music and message directly to them. It is your sweat and genius that made you "low risk" and your "data set" "actionable." All this is now proven out on Excel spreadsheets being passed around oblong conference tables to make other business folks believe slightly more now what they didn't believe at all before.

That you are the motherfucking truth.

And you know all the horror stories of record deals; all the warning, documentarians who were there, NYC cabbies who were not, and you feel in your gut that you really shouldn't take the deal. You feel like you built it and you can keep building it, like these are the same damn people who ignored you for years, that want to *own* your art and you think how can I trust them, how can I do this deal, but you do. In the end you do.

And you know what?

You are absolutely right to.

Why?

Because you need a deal.

Yeah, you fucking do.

Not a Major label deal mind you, not even a traditionally structured record deal (hold on, we are about to get into all that), but that is why you are here, because you need help. Cuz you are at the abyss between hobby and business; poverty and riches (shit, just some rent money and an uncracked iPhone would be nice); between invisibility and validation; outsider and icon and crossing that cavern requires resources and expertise that no single person possesses.

So yeah, you need a deal.

And anyone telling you otherwise has never actually built something successful in this business. Because if they did, guess what, they, at some point, had a fucking deal. And even if it was a shit deal, even if they say they regret and would never do it again, part of their currently successful position is due to that deal. They may now say they hate it, regret it, say they could of done it all on their own, but, guess what? They didn't. They took it, they got some money, some bodies, some resources, learned a ton, mostly the hard way and otherwise and ultimately made it work for them the best they could given their circumstances.

And that's the best you can ever ask for.

Let's look at some deals.

MAJOR LABELS

The main record companies, the big ones, are called Major Labels or "Majors." There are now only three big global conglomerates left and they have their hands on less than 1 percent of the world's musicians.

Wait, if this is a general guide to the future of music business, why are we starting with the antiquated companies controlling a sliver of musicians?

Simple, because this where the majority of the music *commerce* is initiated, thus the business structures set here set the industry "standards" we are learning about and trying to break from. Plus they may have only 1 percent of the musicians, but they have over 70 percent of the world's music product and it remains the holy grail for artists.

Think of Majors as the Royal Swedish Academy of Sciences (they give out the Noble Prize people, come on!). Scientists don't get into science for a Nobel Prize and they don't spend their days in the lab chasing a silly award, but they do want to work with the most cutting edge resources and people in their field. They want to take concepts and ideas, tinker and test and get those hunches and theories and creative tidbits that are floating around their brain out into the world in the way they imagined so that they might make a difference to someone, somewhere, even if that's other scientists who take their discoveries and build.

That's you. That's the Majors.

Putting your personal musical taste aside, this is historically where the majority of the most talented, driven artists get the most financing and recourses to test their theories. And this is where the majority of the money and time is spent taking these theories to market; billions of dollars annually to get sounds from between artists' ears and into fans' ears. Some of it is genius, some duds, some derivative attempts at money and fame. This is not a critique of major label content nor practices (yet), it is just setting the baseline fact the Majors are the NFL of record deals; whether or not you like to watch people give each other concussions is moot.

This may change (that's kinda the point of this book,) but here we are. So let's talk about the Major process, functionally, for you, a typical artist with a dream of having as many people as possible hear and appreciate your work product. Here is how it plays out:

Majors, as we described a moment ago, wait while you go drum up the interest then chase.

This early stage is some insane shit when you think about it. See the Majors wait wait wait until someone, you hopefully, is so undeniably great that everyone in the business is aware and chasing it. Then they woo along side all of the competitors. This collective courtship of course sends the price up and up forcing the eventual victor to commit to overpaying based on the environment of irrationality and exuberance–an environment that they themselves created (by waiting until their target was publicly proven viable). More practically, they are modeling their financial projections and deriving a valuation of the artist and music when that artist is at a peak value. And this peak value, as just described, has been artificially inflated due to their own pursuit of that artist.

Forget your MBA discounted cash flow models—the true valuation of any business is what the market will bear. And public Major label wooing literally causes the market to bear more than is rational.

It's a bubble.

Stock market, dot coms, housing, a bubble is when a price is higher than the actual value based on a flawed confidence of the future value. Every artist, every deal is a bubble, a micro bubble. And this does not even take into consideration the fact that manifesting said future value is based on the non-quantifiable activity we described earlier as "breaking." So Majors make bubbles in markets they don't control and try to get return on that capital in ways they can't define.

Still with me? Lets simplify.

It's like before you go to a used car dealer, you hype up all your friends and bring them along to bid against you when no one was even really sure they needed a car, they just wanted a way to get to where they were going.

Kinda-sorta funny but let's look at the repercussions for the industry at large, this means we quickly transition away from offering an artist who has real potential in the market, a practical based deal based on achievable goals and a rational plan to execute. Instead we offer a deal based on self-propagated hype. The labels enter a win-at-all-costs arena with their largest competitors.

Now the labels, afraid they will never be able get all that money back on recorded music copyright exploitation alone, will demand additional rights over and above music copyright (we will get into "all-rights" deals too) to justify the unjustifiable valuation that they themselves are creating!

Meanwhile all the people feeding at the trough (i.e., managers, lawyers, friends from childhood, relatives the artist never knew they had, me) are now being asked to help advise on a choice between thoughtful, rational, long term career decisions or tens, maybe hundreds of thousands of dollars, in immediate cash commissions and fees based on these irrational valuations. As you can see this is not rocket science nor is this immoral. This is predictable and rationale human behavior. (Minus the part where labels run up their own prices, that part makes no sense.)

Ok so, micro-bubbles, bad deals, insanity, now where does that get us?

It gets you backstage with the one label you can stomach and a hand-shake commitment.

Cool, now what?

Remember those two lawyers? This is when we stick them in a room to battle mercilessly over minutiae like free goods deductions and mechanical caps (don't ask, well, ask, but ask your lawyer). So, the lawyers are lawyering and complaining incessantly as to the idiocy of the other side, on both sides, until both sides claim the other is "IN-SANE!" and everyone is ready to walk. Finally, at this breaking point, a deal is cut as both lawyers remember that they don't want to lose their jobs when everyone else points to them for blowing the deal. Cue the smiles at the steak dinner and now lets go build a business together!

Oh, the steak dinner is recoupable which means YOU ARE PAYING FOR IT. Usually (hopefully) your manager knows this, but doesn't really care because its coming out of your marketing fund, which is not controlled nor commissioned by managers and can always be negotiated higher later anyway. This does not make them a bad person/manager btw; it's a big moment, steak is delicious to most flesh-eaters, everyone is having a great time and life is too short to quibble over a couple hundred bucks and you just signed a record deal, I mean a low risk high yield intellectual property rights deal—woooohooooo!

Oh, oh, the lawyer will add $50k in legal fees, and probably gave a point for it.

Oh, oh, oh, that $50k is also recoupable, i.e., YOU ARE PAYING FOR IT.

Oh, oh, oh, oh, the final fine print says you need to turn in an "approved album," not an "album," so let's hope they "approve" of your music, because god forbid they don't hear a single and tell you we should "try one more" or some other coded phraseology for "fuck, I don't hear a hit on this goddam art project," otherwise good luck going back in the studio to make the music they want i.e., think will sell i.e., not the music you want to make otherwise you would have turned that in in the first place.

Congrats!

Oh, oh, oh, oh, oh, you turned in 14 songs and 3 interludes, so them asking you that just one might possibly be helpful in making money, the money they just gave you, is not a totally egregious ask on their part. And practically, speaking for you, the "hit"—picked by them or you—is the record the label is going to spend the bulk of their money on, is the record that the bulk of fans are going to know and come to your shows to hear and thus will be the record that ends up making you most of your money, both directly from sales and fans at shows and indirectly from endorsement deals, TV ads, etc. And yes, you will likely end up despising that hit song cuz you've had to play it a gajillion times. Sucks, but we are in the major label section baby, now get outta my office kid and go make me some global smash hits baby, yer dynamite!

Wow. Am I sure you need a deal?

Yep. And not because you are a naive artist with a dream, but because you are an entrepreneur with an early stage business venture. Let me repeat that as this builds off the last chapter and is the crux of where we are.

THE CRUX 2.0: You need resources.

Young artist entrepreneurs, you, require three key things: planning, resources, and execution. And this is what you are doing when you do a record deal in the first place, you are capitalizing your business and attempting to scale, i.e., grow, your business from its current level to the next with partners that offer more resources (money is one such resource, publicity is another, etc.) than you possess independently. And just because you don't speak in this vernacular, doesn't mean it is not relevant or true, it just means you need to go get someone who speaks it and put them on your team.

And yes you, your art and thus your business is unique - all businesses differ in their origin, design and goals, but they all grow via the same planning, resources, and execution. Yes, the amount of planning, resources, and execution varies by nature of the business and entrepreneur at the helm, but you need the trifecta. An idea sparks a plan of action, a plan requires resources to pull off, the "pulling off" is called execution. In the artist business, like all businesses, you, the entrepreneur always starts off doing it all themselves. As you grow, your needs grow and you need help.

Major labels are one such form of help.

Define "help"?

Radio and money.

Sure there are added benefits the Majors *can* provide—access to the industries top music makers, a worldwide team of experts working tirelessly to promote your music, some of the brightest most dedicated executives leveraging their thirty years in the business to get you every opportunity to succeed. But these are not guaranteed, radio and money are, better be, better double check with your lawyer.

I know, I know, radio? Really? Still? Yes people. I hate to admit it, but radio matters, not like matters, but like MATTERS. If you are not on it, you don't MATTER. That doesn't mean your music is not amazing (hell, it might actually be, but by amazing I mean pioneering, genre-defying, so ahead of its time it doesn't fit the current format. But, guess what, if so, it will eventually be played on radio, when the masses catch up to your genius). It doesn't mean you can't have a career or are not enjoying one currently; you can *not* be on the radio and survive, make a living, but any artist sustaining a career while not on the radio was either once on the radio or built a brand of radio defiance (see future chapter Brands on Brands on Brands).

Hello punk, lyricist, outlaw country, folk gurus, glitch masters of some cultish sub-genre, I hear you yelling at me through the page, but even you, eschewing the mass pop song repeat machine busy beaming gibberish and nonsensery into our citizenry's earholes (a.k.a., radio), even your successful self proclaimed heroes of art have ended up on the radio at some point in their career. I am not saying it has to be pop radio, I am not saying you have to want it, I am not saying you have to like it, but in the business of music, its fucking undeniably critical. It means large swathes of ordinary citizens like your music. You know how many hits Johnny Cash had on the radio? A hundred and seventy two. I made that up, but it's far from zero and they were sustained over decades.

I got an email from one of my artist's labels the other day about people calling into the radio station in Houston to request their record be played.

What?

Who is still using a telephone to call a radio station to request a song? I mean, flattered for sure and could not be more appreciative, but who does that? People that's who. Lots of people who listen to music, buy music related stuff, go to shows, go online and like and follow and chat and discuss and argue and comment and draw fan art and make lip synch videos and generally are the building blocks for artists careers that's who. People you will point to as justification for that big check from that big brand one day. Radio is not dead, avoid it in the short term at your peril.

Although "alive" is probably not the right term here either.

Radio is a zombie—not alive, not dead, infecting the brains of the masses while trying to adapt to a new body before we humans discover a technological advancement that will kill it off for good. And when we do, whatever broadcast medium replaces it, just reread this section and replace it for the word "radio." I am looking at you "(insert tech media company name) Hits Playlist."

And major labels are hands down the best at working radio. They have the relationships, the expertise, the history, the relationships, the money, the relationships and the relationships as well as the relationships to get you on the radio and the hits playlist. Yes, this requires a great song first. See 3-Step Plan.

Another key resource, and arguably today's most important component of a Major deal is straight cash motherfucking money. This one isn't based on relationships, it doesn't waiver based on human commitment and worker productivity level, you just get it and it's yours. Yes, the funding tied to working (marketing, promotion, etc.) the album over time may be nudged one way or the other due to personal and professional alliances, but Major labels do commit and spend vast sums of money to get their products to market. Deliver a great album and you will get a fair shot, "fair" being defined simply as equal to any other artist on your label.

Now this is not, as some of you believe, free money. It is also not, as some of you believe, soul selling. It is a business transaction. So as with any funding source—local bank to rich uncle to venture capitalist—it does require some security in exchange for them letting you have some of their money. These people, all business people, want a reduction in the risk of never seeing their money again; some level of confidence, some historical precedent, some "metrics," to make them feel good about giving you their money. This is not because they are bad people but because you are asking them to give you their money. Your mom is more likely to put $500 into your music career then a venture capitalist, but not if she has never heard you making music in your room. A VC might invest $5mm, but not if there isn't a strong fundamental business case, reliable team, and clear path to revenue. They are not dicks in the same way your mom is not mean, they are business people; business people who, unlike your mom, don't know you and whose entire job is to make money.

THE CRUX 3.0: A business person's job is to make money.

Nike executives don't make shoes, they make money. Restaurateurs don't make food, they make money. I don't care if the owner is a chef with a lifelong a passion for sustainable gastronomy, they only eat if they earn more than it costs them to plate it. A Major Label executive's job is not to like your music, it's to make money off owned intellectual property assets. And not to make *you* money, but to make the label money. You get money if and when the label makes enough money to pay you (see the fine print of the deal your hopefully great lawyer negotiated for you). So I will never understand all these music people who act surprised and get upset AFTER they accepted cash from multibillion-dollar corporations. Hell, if you put your own money into your music expect to at least pay yourself back!

This is not a nonprofit people.

Remember, you left Aunt Susie's BBQ and put out the tip jar.

The Majors, for now, are still the largest funding source on the planet and have with the most incentive to help you make and sell music. But they are only giving you money in the belief that they will make more money than what they gave you by selling your music. If they want more rights it is because they believe there is a healthy possibility that the money they give you to make music will not be paid back in the form of music sales and licensing alone. If you don't want to give up more rights, then try asking for less money.

Btw, I have done this, taken money OFF the table in a deal to get more favorable rights. I must say it might be worth doing just to watch the Major Label heads explode when you say you want less money. "Did you just say that's *too much* money?!?" BOOOHHHMMM.

Have I mentioned I have been called "crazy" by multiple record execs? I see them every once and a while, strolling around backstage at festivals wearing ripped pants some cute young sales girl convincingly told them they weren't too old for and out of date "luxury" sneakers. Note to reader, if you ever see me like this please immediately rush up to me a slap me in the face, no fist, just open palm, soap opera, embarrassing slap—wait, never mind my artists will for sure beat you to it.

Now don't get too hung up on the deal specifics (just make sure your lawyer does), remember it is just a business transaction that provides a service, a service you need. Make sure you feel good about the PEOPLE who will be working with you to create and exploit your music. After you and the music, they will be most critical in your success—not a few more grand in your pocket or a royalty percentage point. Trust that your attorney makes a great deal and make sure the team around you loves you and would kill for you. Now you're in business, so now you are the CEO, motivate your crew.

Wait, don't other options exist?

Yes, of course, but we are on the part of the book about Major labels, stay focused.

This is a critical point, so let us pause and think back to Crux 2. In the modern music ecosystem artists are entrepreneurs. This is a new development. True, artists have always been the creators of products and services that were to be sold, but the modern twist is that music is no longer what's for sale. Which brings us to Crux 4.

THE CRUX 4.0: It's not about the music, it's what the music is about, which means it's about the music.

Now Crux 4 is some Zen ass shit. I don't want you to have to meditate on it (although you should, a little meditation to keep your head straight in this business will go a long way, see my future book, *Jellyfish Breath - How To Escape Your Own Mind*) you got music to make. So let's break down Crux 4 for a sec before we continue.

"It's not about the music (products people consume), it's what the music is about (the nature in which that music impacts peoples' lives), which means it's about the music (impacting peoples' lives via your art)." Which is the same as it's always been, just different.

See our business has *always* been about developing music and artists in an attempt to leverage said music to sell products and services. Merch to concerts to TV specials to Greatest Hits album packages to private events to speaking engagements to sponsorships, we have always been relying on the power and reach of great artists' great music to increase our income streams.

Yes, the industry's primary product, music, has experienced a permanent reduction in value, but that does not mean the businesses is *less* reliant on great music, it means great music matters *MORE* than ever!

When we were building Beats by Dre Headphones at Interscope Records the common refrain from people who didn't understand why a record label was getting into the consumer electronic space business was "there would be no Beats by Dre without Dre". This was said as if we were devaluing the music in the equation, but that's where things are misunderstood. Look, if you want to make a song and sell that song for $0.99 that better be a really good song. If you want to make a song and get a hundred million clicks online that better be really, really good song. If you want to make a song and use it to sell $400.00 headphones, that better be the greatest fucking song ever in a catalog full of great fucking songs.

See, the magic of music as a product was born with music boxes in the eighteen century. It started with consumer technology that needed content. The phonograph was iterative. The magic of music today is not iterative product, but a radical redefining of what it means to create value with music i.e., the ability for an artist to create art at such a level of significance that it modifies the very existence of other human beings. To then make a plan to capitalize on some of that value is not devaluing music, its giving music the proper respect that it is due. Headphones are simply one creative way for one creative artist to extract more of *their* value. Every artist creates some level of value, its on you, us, to figure out what it is and go get it back. If you stop to think about it objectively, music as product is the devaluation of music!

Music stripped from its format, pulled out of the artist's intended sequence and restructure to be streamed in a playlist with a bunch of other random records, that is the devaluation of music. That is how you lose the essence and soul and intention of music.

Yes I am biased. Yes I am a strategy guy attempting to help build music's next evolutionary playground. But don't tell me that an artist, attempting to retain the fundamental value of their work output is devaluing their art. Their output moves consumers, moves companies, moves markets—to attempt to own this impact is not only not devaluation, it is the fundamental objective of all companies i.e., find a niche wherein one is uniquely positioned to fill an unserved consumer need and leverage ones expertise to sustain an advantage and scale.

Nike sells the shoes you are wearing in your video and its lauded a bold and innovative business move. But you, the artist, dare to make and wear your own brand of shoes and you are deemed a "sell out" who "should focus on the music"? Fuck that.

Ok, now I am ranting and digressing, let's get back to, wait, one more anecdote.

I have an artist who wrote a song about a friend's suicide. The song was on the shortlist for a commercial and I sat around a conference table listening to ad executives and their young assistants who had their "finger on the pulse" debate the effectiveness of this song, this piece of my friend's soul to sell their sneakers.

I wanted to scream. I wanted to punch someone in the neck. I wanted to storm out. But my artist friend hadn't bought groceries in a month and only thing his soul will let him do with is make music. And I mean this ad placement could have been enough to "break" him. He could have got a nice check and a kickstart to a tour, maybe a label look and be that much closer to making a living off his art. And that's the dilemma. Everyone wants to comment on what is "appropriate" for an artist to do to make a living, while all the companies making a living off of artists art are immune from criticism.

And I guess that's the point of this Crux 4 digression, I don't care if you are Dr. Dre or my friend or some kid in your basement, if you wish to have a career in music, then you are in business of music and so you must not simply matter in the ears of people but your art must permeate the lives of those who hear it. And if and when it does it is up to you to get your full value for your greatness. See great music possesses people. Changes people. Triggers emotions and exposes feelings we didn't know we had.

Music's true value is the visceral connection it makes with other humans.

So why are we getting into this in the middle of Major Label talk? Because *music* is now the driver of a broad-based business of assets and services and Major Labels control the vast majority of music. And because your music is more important than ever, getting the help you need making that music great and getting that music to the largest possible base of listeners is ever more critical. Majors do more of that commercially, currently, than anyone else.

Plus I didn't want to get too far down the "record deal" path and not address how important it is for you to understand the full range of impact the music you make makes.

Let's get out of this Zen philosophical crap about what music is about and take a look at what these Major Label deals are about. All of the industry record deals are patterned off of these, so we'll dive in here.

THE CLASSIC DEAL

The all time classic hall of fame record deal is the "royalty deal." Not the best, not the worst, increasingly less popular as the industry standard, but we are going dive deep here as it is foundation on which all other deals are based.

A royalty deal is fairly simple (as long as you don't read the fine print on page 75 of the final long form document) structure in which the artist gets a cash "advance" up front to live on while they make an album. It is a recent phenomenon that the "advance" is seen as a badge of honor, something rappers brag about and artists thinking of as income. Think of an advance as an interest free loan lent based on a finance department's projection of your future earnings. Think about it this way because that is exactly what it is. Of course, it may become hyperinflated given our latest bubble discussion, but have no doubt there is an excel spreadsheet in a pile of papers somewhere with the exact number of sales, streams, and licenses needed to earn back your loan plus a percentage.

Your percentage will be around 16 percent. I have seen as low as 12 percent as high as 22 percent. These, your royalty earnings, are calculated and paid on net receipts. Not gross receipts mind you, "net", which in laymen terms means after someone has taken a little something off the top so be sure find that smart and savvy math pro for your team.

Profit split deals exist too, but these are really just royalty deals with a different defined calculation. All payouts are part of overly complex written legally binding calculation so you can be sure the label has thought through the loss of profitability by defining your royalty as a profit and compensated for that in the definition. No need to dive too far in here as they work exactly how they sound—you split profits with the label. And again, insert knowledgeable team here.

In exchange for the advance the contract will specify that the label now owns all recordings you are make during the term of your contract. Any and all. By definition this does not just include the ones that will eventually make your album, but any records you make over that term, so again, and you know what I am going to say, insert knowledgeable team here pretty please and be mindful on publicly voicing your prolific-ness.

Lets get into some language.

The TERM is the length of time you are contractually obligated to work with the label, you can expect an ask of at least a one plus one "1 + 1." That is one album and (we say "plus", I don't know why) an OPTION for another one album. This means you are obligated to deliver to the label two albums, one for sure plus another one if they ask. Key word being "they." It is an "option", but it is *always* the labels option. Now, they do have to pay you for the option album if they choose to pick up, but that will all be spelled out up front, in some crazy confusing formula full of contingencies that a bunch of legal and quant guys make up trying to out-wit each other, I mean, adeptly negotiate your record deal.

The committed term varies by deal, but typically sits between 1 + 1 and a 1 + 3 (obligation to deliver 1 album plus 3 individual options for the label to require you to deliver up to 4 total albums). Again, this can be anything: 1 firm for those acts setting their own terms; 2 + 2 for a credible band the label knows it wants to keep around; 1 + 6 for an unknown entity with a hot song and no history.

That's my favorite soulless label overreach btw, the 1 + 6; it essentially locks an artist up for life on the cheap while at the same time proving the label has no real commitment to, confidence in or desire to keep you around. The 1 + 6 is basically dynamite fishing.

Oh, helpful hint, do not ever sign anything over a 1 + 2 and make sure the options are expensive enough to make the label really think before picking it up. Remember, these options are the label's option so you want them to truly commit, not just ask for another option because it's cheap enough to eliminate the risk of you going somewhere else and making a great record without them. The cash commitment is your safeguard, they are a corporation, the only way to ensure a corporation takes something seriously is to have a substantial monetary impact associated with the decision. You also don't want them to overpay and be so upset as to not work your LP properly, you want them just nervous enough to work hard. Let your great lawyer handle this part.

A key consideration that is often overlooked is the ALBUM CYCLE, or the length of time between the date your album releases and the date the next album will release. The historical norm is 2 years-ish, but this is dropping in the digital age as both the time needed to record and the attention span of the public is dropping so let's call it 18 months. First and foremost the album cycle needs to be long enough for you to properly "work the record" i.e., actively support your album in the marketplace i.e., market, promote, play shows, etc. i.e., do all those things you need to do make sure people are aware that your music exists and have a chance to listen to it long enough to have an opinion. Again, herein we are working off the assumption that you are pouring your soul into art people can hear so it would follow that a dedicating an ample period of time and attention to have people listen would be a positive.

This seems like a no-brainer on both sides, but labels are quick to jump off a single that is not working and artists are equally as quick to drop free music on the internet if their album is not receiving timely feedback. A reminder to both sides: we live in the new age of the endless stimulating digital content sea, give that music a chance to swim.

There also needs to be an ample amount of time for you to have enough personal growth as to warrant another complete body of work. You want your fans to miss you, but not forget you. This is not to say you won't release more music in between—free songs, cover songs, b-sides, demos—but this will all be based on personal desire and/or marketing. Again, we are in the classic deal section, maybe you are early Lil B level prolific and get a smart squad and negotiate non-traditional singles or streaming deals, but we aren't there yet. We are on deal fundamentals and rationale.

Now this downward pressure on the album cycle is not necessarily a bad thing. In the albums' golden age, the 1960s, the great acts released an album every year. But it was an album i.e., 10-ish correlated original musical works, not an EP (extended play, meaning longer then a single, but not a LP, long play, album) or a mixtape (some blend of original music and lyrics arranged with existing musical material release for free, free because if you use music you don't own and try to sell it you can/will be sued by those that own it). Neither the EP nor mixtape count towards the albums you commited to deliver to the label.

Now let's not confuse album cycle with a traditional business person's "product lifecycle." A product lifecycle follows a product from inception through development, marketing, release, sales and to its end of life. An album's product lifecycle can be anywhere from three months to sixty years. Flop to classic, but I use both terms loosely. Those lucky enough to be part of the latter your product will be managed across multiple record label divisions, depending on its phase of life. The actual record label you sign to will manage the album from creation/delivery through the album cycle and then hand it/ you off to the "catalog" division a.k.a., the retirement home for albums, where old music goes to die and/or be visited occasionally by people with some level of personal connection.

I will let you handle the management of your catalog, if you are lucky enough to have one you will hopefully no longer need this book!

As you can now see even with a reduced cycle time and low option commitments the length of your deal adds up quickly. A short 1 + 1 could be as long as five years assuming it takes you a year to finish and release your first record and then you work it for two years (which is completely reasonable). As noted a 1 + 6 with this logic is basically your whole life.

Lets recap. In a royalty deal you are selling your music for your own money upfront. You are selling the rights to the intellectual property asset that is your music, for an advance against your earning potential. Theoretically, you are paid the amount of money you would have otherwise earned if you just waited and got the royalty paid from the sales. So if you take the money you can't complain later that someone else owns and controls your music—that is literally the deal you just made. And you can't complain that you never see any more money, because the point of a label finance guy, which I have been, is to properly forecast all of the money that your royalty will likely generate and then pay you that up front. And yes, that money is less than it would be if you owned the asset outright and sold the same amount yourself, but theoretically you did the deal precisely because you believed you couldn't sell that much on your own and could earn more money with a label that paid you a lower rate per transaction but transacting infinitely more times.

Reminder, I am not debating the merits here, this is just how it functions.

It's not up to the label to give you a fair deal, it's up to you to understand how the business you say you want to be in works, know your worth, surround yourself with people that know more than you how to quantify that worth, and fight to make a great deal for you. If you do not have that great team or do not have access to a group of savvy folks for hire DO NOT DO THIS DEAL.

And yes you, you who doesn't know anyone in the business yet, you can get a great team. I can promise you if a Major label is ready to offer you a deal there are competent people that will be willing to work with you, so pause, take a breath and go find them.

Don't know where to start?

Google your favorite band and see who represents them legally. Three minutes on the digital interwebs and you will find an office phone number and I guarantee when you explain your situation some junior manager and/or legal assistant, someone in their office will get on the phone with you. If they don't, fuck 'em, call the next one.

Another key to the record business: you don't get what you don't ask for.

Remember, Major labels operate on fear-based decision making— that means if they want to do a deal, it's because they think someone else might get to you first. And they are correct in thinking that. They were incorrect for not offering you a deal earlier, but again, if they had, then their decision making would not be fear based, which it is. Bottom line is that does not matter how much work you have done, how much "proof" you have provided, how good you are or whether or not the majority of the folks at the label even truly believe you are good, it all comes down to whether or not they think someone else might scoop it first. Until they so, they will never offer you a deal.

So don't go out trying to "get" a deal. And be weary of anyone who claims they can "get you" a deal. You can't. They can't. All you can do is make people care. And you do that by making luck. And you do that by making music. Do all that and the deals will come.

More deals.

THE ALL RIGHTS DEAL
A.K.A., THE 360

The "all rights" deal, or "the 360" as its affectionately known, is the personification of an industry completely in the dark as to what the fuck they are doing. It is the ultimate fear-based decision. The 360 is the cousin of modern deep sea fishing, its just dragging a giant net across an artist income streams and seeing what you can collect—money, trash, dolphins. We as an industry will look back on these deals in embarrassment.

So to clarify, an "all rights" deal is when a label advances you money to make an album, as in the classic deal scenario, but it earns its money back from sharing a percentage of incoming across all of an artists activities not just the IP asset i.e. touring, merch, stickers, appearances, whatever they can get. Generally this falls below the record royalty, say 5 to 10 percent, but I have seen as much as 25 percent. Again, the percentage will vary based on the stage of your career, negotiating position, and the strength of your team.

Now, in the label's defense, they can provide extremely valuable, and in some cases essential, services for building your broader career. They market and promote your music, your record and because all great artist careers are rooted in the great music they make, labels, by default, are promoting you. The promotion of you and your music is what will become your brand as a whole. Labels do not simply push songs and albums to stores, especially now as sales have been replaced by streams and subscriptions; they provide support and promotion while on the road touring (fliers, banners, radio contests, geo-targeted digital ads), set you up with press (radio, TV, blogs, magazines), maybe book a private show or a speaking engagement or endorsement deal. It's not just about marketing the LP, but about marketing you and your life as an artist. Yet in classic deals the labels do not participated in any revenue other than record sales.

Why not? Because the lion's share of revenue used to come from recorded music and the labels were intent on keeping it. Unfortunately for the labels, this is increasingly not the case. The 360 is an attempt for the labels to recapture some of the value they are creating in the market. All good, I am not mad at the attempt, you just can't ask for more money for doing the same work and that's true in any business.

But it is not just the label's fault. These 360 deals are just more proof of the misalignment of incentives across the business. Even if you and the label could coalesce around a cooperative brand development model in the current industry structure, everyone involved would be affected. More specifically, everyone's *pay* would be affected by decisions that are out of their direct control. That's a huge issue when dealing with "all rights" cuz "all rights" means "all income" and "all income" is controlled and shared by "all parties."

This is a good time for a quick breakdown of how "all parties" share "all income."

Labels get paid from any use of their recordings. ("Their" meaning the ones they bought into.)
Publishers get paid from any use of their lyrics and music. ("Their" meaning the ones they bought into.)

Managers get paid from a percentage on everything an artist earns throughout the entertainment industry.

Agents get paid a percentage on touring income and any name/likeness-based deals they can bring to the table.

Lawyers get paid from of all income requiring a contract i.e., 99 percent of everything. You can pay a percentage of gross income or hourly.

Business managers a.k.a., accountants, get paid from anything flowing into the artists business account. Here as well you can pay a percentage of gross income or hourly.

PR, PA's, photographers, video directors, etc. are all hired guns.

Why percentages? Well this is how everyone gets paid for all the "free" (i.e., not billed to the artist and not salaried employees) hours of work people on your team are doing helping run the broader business i.e., all these income streams. These relationships and contracts differ, but the above are pretty standard. This pay structure is a bit like traditional start up entrepreneurs who "pay" for work by giving equity since they do not have cash. Starting artists down have much either. For example, you can't pay $200-$500 hourly legal fees to do your tour contracts so you trade 5 percent of earnings—a great deal for you in short term, terrible deal for you in the long term.

Sidenote: Two things you do not skimp on in this business are lawyers and accountants. These people determine how you get your money, what you own, what you owe, how you are protected. That protection includes your friend, manager, and yourself. What you own is your art, your art is your money. Don't fuck around with your money.

Managers are theoretically aligned most with the artists, but even there the industry has found work arounds. For example manger's commission income in the form of advance payments, but do not commission working capital e.g., tour support, A&R funds (money to make records), etc. So guess what happens next? The commissionable parts like advances get bigger, non-commissionable parts like label services get smaller. Managers are aligned, but they are human. Remember, these humans work FOR you.

So why would anyone do these 360 deals in the current form? Honestly, I don't know. I would happily do some form of all-rights deal and actually believe that it would be of value to all parties IF the label was willing to provide funding for and dedicate services against the non-record revenue streams. After all, a team fully aligned around a core set of measurable incentives is always the best path forward for any business. That's just not how it ends up working.

At Interscope, I was involved in some of the first ever multi-right deals, what would eventually become the "360," and I can say that it was never intended to be a money grab. Our crew was advocating for a more "venture capital" based investment approach, where we would fund additional capital to develop artist specific ancillary businesses that we felt were uniquely positioned to help scale. We felt if we could invest more in our artists and their teams, specifically supporting businesses in the markets that our artists were passionate about and had a measurable level of impact, we would be in a great position to grow in a new, mutually beneficial partnership structure. (This was eventually to become the foundation of my company 3QTR.) It was never as simple as good ideas and good partnerships, but we had been seeding and launching these types of businesses for years i.e., apparel, hardgoods, beverage, technology start-ups; we even started management firms, tour companies, branding companies. This was the result of top down driven, multi-year sustained innovation efforts; not luck, not greed, it was R&D. It's just not called R&D in the music business.

I fundamentally believe that a music company that funds, supports, and operates in a transparent partnership with an artist to develop the totality of their business with the artist as CEO is the path forward. Whoever fills the management team is up to the artist, but just as it's the artist job to be a world class creative, the management team should have world class skills in business and brand development. And I do not say "management team" in the traditional artist-manager sense, I say it in the executive business management sense. You don't need a trusted friend to sit in rooms for you, field incoming calls, and scour for more income opportunities. While those are all artist business functions, if you do not have a manager that is operating in a COO capacity i.e., strategically operating the totality of your business for the long term then you are putting yourself at risk. Great music, like any great product, can fill in the gaps and help sustain you in the short term i.e., when that music is being listened to and relevant in the immediate culture, but it cannot sustain you long term. Just look back to that list of players earning a living off of the artist—agent, label, publisher, etc.—in addition to managing all-rights, someone has to manage all of those relationships and incentive structures.

Again, there are exceptions that you can count on one hand, where

100

music just wins the day. I love it, but you don't base your career on anomalies. Plus, these artists have also lived in a past world where copyright law and proper oversight yielded proper payment for use i.e., they are still getting large royalty checks for songs they wrote thirty years ago. We no longer live in that world. I too hope we return, but, this is not that book.

Oh, quickly on the "anomalies" – my favorite example I give my artists is Michael Jordan. Freakish talent and in the running for basketball's GOAT (greatest of all time). But not from talent, from using talent as the starting point to work from. Three MVPs in and the guy is still the first one in the gym and last one out. Shooting free throws. The most base level, boring, fundamental skill. Kobe, Lebron, Curry insert your pick for GOAT here and I bet you they are all the same. Talent gets your foot in the door, drive, work, ambition, team get you to "anomaly" status.

Ok, so why are we discussing this here in the all-rights section? Because you need to realize how important it is to manage "all" of your "rights." Look, I agree that this is not the fun, free-swinging business you dreamt of when you headed into music, but it's where we are. Fortunately, the better the team around you, the more you get to stay in the creative lane. The greatest artists have the best teams worrying about this shit. They are out changing the world and they have entrusted great people to handle and report back. Like a great CEO.

Now there is likely a whole book to be written on the how's and why's of an egalitarian partnership model designed to evolve the business morphed into the modern net drag "360," but for our purposes lets just chalk it up to a history of mutual mistrust coupled with corporate politics that are not going to be remedied by a few months of presenting rational arguments to people still making multi-million dollar decisions in a multi-billion dollar market based on the number of times someone uses a telephone to request one of their products be played for free via a one hundred year old electromagnetic broadcasting technology.

So we should all go independent right?

INDEPENDENT LABELS

Oh Indies, here is where I am supposed to purport my undying affection for the bastion, nay, beacon, nay utopian society of artists making art for art lovers to art to. This is where I name drop and get all the music heads to rally around me and carry the anti-flag to the castle.

But guess what?

The vast majority of independent labels are just less well-endowed Majors. Indies typically operate under the same backwards, traditional business model as the Majors, but without the money or resources to execute at the Major level.

So the guys (yes, I mean men, 99 percent of the time its 99 percent dudes) running it wear cooler clothes and throw parties at the office and claim to be fans of more of the same music as you do, yes this is all true, you likely have more in common with these people, but who gives a fuck? How is this relevant to being competent at one's chosen vocation? This is a business transaction not a date. We are trying to increase, to any nth degree, the gajillion-to-one odds you have that the music you make and ideas in your head will actually pave the way for a career in music.

And true, often times indies are better (maybe we're soul mates!), but it's not because they are cooler it's because they typically give more fucks about your art, give you 100 percent creative control and are much more efficient and effective at an early stage of an artists career then any Major (more on this is in a moment).

Cuz let's look at specifics: an indie is going to pay you a smaller amount of advance money, but is still going to own your masters. Let me repeat that. That cool guy with the beard, tats, drinking the recently newest fashionable old cheap beer brand to replace the last fashionable old cheap beer brand is going to *own your masters* by *paying you less money*. Subsequently this indie going try to monetize your record. How? Via the exact same channels and 99 percent of the same methodology as a Major label. And they are gonna do it with less resources.

Or as my southern dirt-track racing artist constituency taught me "all show and no go."

How do suppose that is going to work out for you?

So bad indies are the same as bad Majors just using the counter argument to win your business i.e., you need small, targeted, hands-on v. a global, heavily resourced, machine.

I know, yeah, genius advice, you don't need to do bad deals with bad people. So what do great indies do?

Great indies leverage their position outside the mainstream system and rulebook and use it to make waves in the market. They bring attention to the nuances and craftsmanship of your art, creative process and the inherent ingenuity you have as an artist. They place bets that your ideas and the way you want to present your art is the best way to do so; then they get behind and compliment that vision. (Hmmm, sounds like what a great CEO does?) All things that a formulaic Major system does not allow for. When this happens indies are amazing for artists at any stage. That is assuming you are a nuanced craftsman with an ingenious nature, which, for purposes of this paragraph, we shall assume that you are.

One key benefit of indies is it is easier to cut more artist friendly deals. Remember that insane wooing process? Not applicable here. Indies have the freedom to be much more discerning in their A&R process. They can and do, of course, overlap with Majors, but indies have the freedom to seek out and sign music that moves them and potentially smaller subset of fans then the entire music listening population on planet Earth.

So eliminate the crazy run up to signing, then you eliminate the insane closed-door lawyering and you get direct artist involvement and with the actual contractual parties at the table it makes sense you would get more realistic partnerships. Now this is not to say there is a higher likelihood of "success," but kicking off a deal where people feel not-victimized by the other party is generally speaking a good starting point.

Financially, with the smaller advance and more hands on dialogue from you and the label, a profit split arrangement is more typical; wherein, as mentioned, instead of a small royalty on net receipts, you get paid 50 percent of net profits. However, these are calculated via the same "total earnings" projection that the Majors use so it the advance will still be based on the money everyone expects you to earn anyway. And with less money and less resources going into your project profits are generally just fleeting as royalties.

And maybe you can keep your masters. More and more indie deals are structured as a license—7, 10, 15 years—and then the master recordings revert to your ownership. There is a lot that goes into this, including, most commonly, a formula that says they only revert after the time period AND the label earning all their money back plus a percentage. This is all negotiable however, and the fact that is on the table is a huge plus. Even if you are not making a bunch of money from them, they are your songs and if nothing else, owning your own work is gonna feel good at any stage. Again, as with Majors, insert savvy lawyer here.

The other key benefit here is of course retaining creative control. With an indie you can typically make the record you want to make, of primary importance to any artist. Huge win on the face of it, but again, this partner is supposed to be selling your work and making you money and developing your career so their absence of input is a great thing if they are meddling, obstructionist, musically devoid assholes (which some are), but not such a great thing if they are smart and musically savvy folks with good ideas (which some are).

Further, their ideas are most certainly cooler, they are most certainly more relevant to a cooler, trendset-ier i.e., non-mass-market audience, so if that's your fan-base there is real value in having them work your record. Could be forever or even just as a stepping stone to that next level when the mass is within reach and/or you have a desire to reach out.

However remember, cooler people do cooler shit on all levels not just marketing ideas, so when you are all out drinking beer on Wednesday afternoon that means no one is at the office working your fucking record. So yes, you gotta love cool people with the passion to put the music first, I am just saying that that alone is not of a logical rationale for putting someone in charge of your core business. And given that many indies the literally offer you the same deal and services as the classic major deal discussed do not be naively drawn into the hypnosis of cool.

I say this the same way I say that Majors giving you a lot of money is alone not a logical rationale for putting someone in charge of your core business. Vet your options well.

And you need a deal, remember?

And you are the CEO of your own future remember?

See an indie deal may feel more "free" from business-y type stuff, but the truth is less resources means that more of the business stuff will fall on you and your team which is even more in line with the CEO talk I have been doing. I hate to harp on it, but there is a certain level of unavoidable business that needs to get done in the music business, so if your label partner is not doing that stuff, then you are doing that stuff.

Let's examine.

If you have more options for partners (there are more indies then majors) you need to be more discerning in your choice and thus have a better idea of what to look for in said label partner. If you have more leeway in deal structure and pulling the levers then you need to know even more about what you want and the levers required to get it. If you have more of a say in how to market and promote your album then you better know how to market and promote an album. If you have low/no input in album making then you need to know how to make and deliver a great album, a.k.a., you gotta get and stay smarter.

So the spectrum of artists and labels is infinite—you just need to be honest with yourself where on that spectrum you find yourself. And if you want to progress, you need to align yourself with the appropriate resources to do so.

But, you say, what if you find an indie with the passion and business acumen and an appropriate level of cash? Holy grail right? Yes, absolutely, and there are some out there I have worked with and are amazing. But the reciprocal is also true, a Major deal that allows for creative control is also amazing. (I have yet to hear of an all-rights deal worth doing.)

Look, the only constant is you need great people around you. Find them and do the best deal you can.

Wait, if we are all CEOs and we are just need great people, we should all go DIY right?

DIY

DIY is a myth.

DIY is a tech buzzword employed to by alternative digital media outlets who would prefer that you use their suite of services and platforms instead of the traditional ones. Not because they are evil technologists or bitter ex-label people, but because they don't make money off the old distribution path, they make it off the new one they created and are now trying to sell you on.

Lesson five: There is no such thing as DIY.

Someone has to do the work. One person cannot possibly operate a global business by themselves. And this is what the music business is–a DJ alone in bedroom, a rock band on the road, a rapper on You-Tube, a folk kid in a cabin. Once you upload something online the global consumption of your product begins. Again, you may treat this process with as much or as little structure, seriousness, commerce, art, aloofness as you wish, but you are in business. I don't care if it's two views on YouTube or a Twitter account with no tweets, your art is now part of the commercial ecosystem. And if your goal is, as it should be, to have as many people be exposed to and hopefully moved by your art than this path is going to take some concentrated effort.

One person cannot be the product manufacturer, marketer, salesmen, distributor, promoter, financier, and accountant, and then repeat that across the multiple verticals of live performance, music sales, merchandising, branding tech, etc. This is why you employ, partner, and/or leverage the people that can be most effective in helping you grow your business. Technological advances have automated some of the process, platforms may now be leveraged, but that is not DIY, that is just employing the most efficient tools at your disposal to operate your business.

You may make music in your basement, but you are not pouring hot plastic into vinyl molds down there while you do customer service upgrades to the streaming service you just invented.

And even when you think you are DIY, do you:

Market using social media? The social media companies make money.

Make your own videos? Another social media company makes money.

Sell music direct to fans? The website, platform, software co (SAAS) makes money.

Sell merch direct? The website, platform, the software service makes money.

Now go live a life of rich experience, write songs, make melodies, buy gear, play music, sing, engineer, mix, master, perfect your craft, design art, develop strategy, research, make marketing plans, be witty, often, post, often, take photos, upload, buy shirts, buy ink, manufacture, walk to post office and mail stuff, make videos, set up interviews, do interviews, do photoshoots, promote, get on radio, visit radio stations across the world, book shows, plan travel, get visas, play shows, do ads, get licenses, negotiate contracts, sell, do customer service, file taxes in every place you earned money, coordinate it all in a strategic and efficacious manner, execute, repeat, repeat, repeat.

In truth, there is no DIY strategic plan save busking.

So let's just focus on the music.

If you make great music it will get heard. I am serious. I know it seems impossible, but remember my 3-Step Plan. I know the odds, I am immersed in the noise, but I am telling you they will find you. There are fans out everyday looking for you. There are business people out everyday looking for you. Don't worry about better marketing tactics or sales tricks in the early days, worry about making great music because great music cuts through, great always does.
Music wins and that's the only DIY you need.

So be DIY until you are DIY + your best friend. And then DIY + your best friend + a handful of early believers. And cherish those early believers as they are the fucking greatest most important people on the planet. And be proud of yourself when its just you. And build yourself and keep as much as close to you as long as you possibly can, just don't make the mistake of thinking you can make it completely on your own. Be proud of your bedroom DIY, but also be proud of yourself when "DIY" means assembling a world class team of people and partners around you and bringing your music to the world. I don't care if you are Warren Buffet or Radiohead or the guy who runs both of the mini marts down the street, you don't build the empire yourself, and that's ok.

In truth the spectrum of labels deals looks like this:

EXHIBIT 1. FREEDOM V. RESOURCES

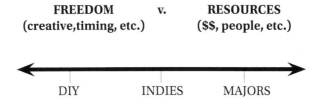

Pick a spot people. This is not rocket science.

NONTRADITIONAL DEALS

As the name implies there are deals that lie outside the traditional label deal landscape. While still rare, they are increasingly being struck due specifically to current market dynamics i.e., shrinking returns in a consolidated market causing those who operate within the old paradigm i.e., the selling of recorded music and traditional tangential products, to shrink. Couple this with an increase in the number of artists seeking services in the new paradigm i.e., brand-based service development rooted in music and you get "nontraditional" players. This still represents a small fraction of professional artist deals, ("professional" as defined by those who's primary source of income is from music related activities while managing to exist above the poverty line). However, given the imbalance in market conditions, any economist will tell you, outside players will enter the market. Lets see if there is way we can synch up high school economic theory with the complexity of today's artist choice.

If the number of people demanding services increases while the number of firms supplying these services decreases, there is a supply problem.

If the service being supplied by a decreasing number of suppliers is inadequate while the number of people and complexity of services being demanded are both increasing, there is a fucking supply problem.

We have a fucking supply problem.

Enter the nontraditional "third party." In music this refers to any non-music company offering to cover creation, marketing, and/or promotion costs of music/music product for free. The offers are pretty much the same across the board—free studio time, free promotion, some shows, and you don't need a label so you keep ownership of your master recordings. For example, a shoe company gives you time in the brick warehouse they turned into a perfectly Instagramable studio in the neighborhood they are gentrifying which you get to use to record if you promise to Instagram that you're doing so in their shoes, hashtag DIY.

Do not confuse this with bartering, as money will most certainly change hands. Typically it comes in the form of reimbursement for expenses incurred during the project e.g., studio, travel, and meals and not flat cash, but that's all to be negotiated.

The exception to not getting a cash payment is if you are asked to perform. Note to the new players, this payment will be requested from you at a reduced rate and will take place in front of a smaller crowd they will characterize as "intimate." Tickets are rarely sold to these events which is great as that would interfere with your regular touring schedule, but it's not for your benefit, it's for theirs—it's so they can have a private event for employees, clients, friends of employees and a few lucky fans that are able to RSVP. Of course the RSVP is simply to allow the third party company that is offering you this deal to market and promote their brand to your audience under the guise that they care about you and your fans, but I mean they are a corporation and are paying you money so you gotta kinda expect it. The big thing to be aware of is these are a *DRAG* to play. Why? Cuz all the vibe in the room will be artificially created by that non-cool company's marketing department. How do I know they are not cool? Cuz they need to pay you to make them look cool. And given that no (or a few token) true fans will be there it will be a low/no energy show. It's more a scene than a show, but again, all good, it's not that it's a bad show, it's a paid corporate job, just part of the deal *IF* you choose to accept it.

Again, these deals are new and all custom so these are generalizations, but one thing you can be sure of is that "free" actually means licensing your name, likeness and music both live and recorded for use in their promotional campaigns.

And do not confuse this with endorsement deals, wherein a third party brand pays you cash to advertise for them. An endorsement deal is not music related, it's celebrity related. That's a straight-up deal to use you to reach consumers. Not saying it's good or bad, it's just super clear cut so everyone knows upfront what they are getting into, see future chapter Brands on Brands on Brands.

Now third party deals are the most commonly struck by Fortune 500 brands that fancy themselves in the "youth culture" and/or "lifestyle" business. Or rather some ungodly number of focus groups have convinced them that they need to matter more to younger people. Now these firms believe their best chance at recapturing some of that lost pixie dust / mojo is to get hip with the kids. Apparently I missed the day of business school where the professor in my Fucking Supply Problems class, a.k.a., Econ 307, scribbled on the white board the famous equation: hip kids + product = growth.

Note to these firms, your company does not suck because kids think it sucks, kids think it sucks because it sucks. The only way to remedy this is to make it not suck. But before you go and try to make it not suck, remember it doesn't suck just cuz kids think it sucks. More Zen for you, go ahead meditate on it.

As an artist, it's easy to spot these firms as they will be armed with Powerpoint decks littered with words like "culture," "social," "super-star," "viral," "breakthrough," "impossible," and "tomorrow." Lots of big bold colorful type and charts. There will definitely be a wave and an explosion somewhere in the graphic. Someone on their team will have visible tattoos and that will not be the one with the word "creative" in their title.

In all seriousness, these are dangerous deals.

Deals when a multinational conglomerate offers you something for free is, by definition, bullshit. If that multinational conglomerate offers you something for free, while at the same time insisting that it has your best interest at heart? This is Grade A, motherfucking-smiling-cow-on-the-frozen-bag-of-meat bullshit. Cuz let's be clear, multinational conglomerates don't bullshit; they make vast sums of money, so you can safely assume if there's bullshit its only for one of the parties step in.

Poker 101 people, if you're in a game ten minutes and don't see a sucker, you're the sucker.

And I know their pitch sounds convincing. That's because they are a multinational conglomerate. And one does not scale a business to become a multinational conglomerate with so much free cash and time that it believes it both rational and share-holder-accretive to start dabbling in music unless they are dam good at doing things like creating compelling pitches. But you know what they don't do?

Music.

And you know this is true because their job is to maximize cash and if they were great at making cash from music then they would be in the music business and not selling candy-coated widgets that need cool music people like you to stand next to and convince kids to buy said candy-coated widgets. Remember when Coke put out records for that jam band? Unfortunately I do.

The larger issue is not that you are entrusting the core of your business to someone who does not know your business (which is less than ideal), but that you are now part of *their* business. Studio time is in their branded studio that they built as part of *their* marketing plan, promo is part of *their* product advertising, paid shows are commercials for *their* brand and of course you keep the masters, because they are not in the business of selling your products. They are in the business of selling *their* products. And guess what? Now you are in the business of selling *their* products. And you are too busy living a life on the brink of success and failure to being doing other people's work.

This seems obvious, but let's dive into the consequences. You work for them. It may feel freeing and cool, but that's just the money in your pocket and ego at seeing your face on the wall. You are a musician, an artist and you are pouring your life story and emotive output into marketing some random corporations wares. Worse, your art is being used as the facade that this company in some way gives a fuck

116

about the customers, your fans, whose culture, integrity and wallets they are going on to pillage. I mean if your debut music is presented to the world on the Mercedes-Benz Mixed Tape (actual thing) how much more serious am I supposed to take you than the new G Class coupe?

Yes, this may also be true of an endorsement deal, advertising song license, but those are transactions all parties, including your fans, understand and it is up to you to decide if its right for the business on a case by case basis (again, Brands on Brands on Brands chapter forthcoming). Further, these are remnants of a traditional business we are trying to evolve.

Simply put, nontraditional brand deals are not record deals.

And if every record deal is a bad deal, every third party deal is a potential career ender.

This is not in defense of the labels—their innovative ineptitude is the reason we are here. And if the labels continue to fail to find a solution we may live in a world where these deals are much more common. But lets play this out for a sec.

Theoretically, less choice for artists and more availability of these types of deals should cause more artists to accept them, thus providing artists a stronger voice inside these third party businesses. It would follow that artists would gain more power incrementally and begin to cut more advantageous deals. And the third parties would concurrently gain expertise and understanding of artists and music and thus, presumably, become better partners. All of which would begin to resemble a more equitable arrangement for the creators.

This may sound like fantasy, non-music-corporations getting honestly more concerned about artists well being, but it is logical sequence of events given a proper set of variables set in motion by the refusal of traditional music companies to evolve. Lots of "ifs" in there, but you are already starting to see more artist friendly deals due to savvy artists and teams who already understand what I wrote in this section. Evolution is happening, but evolution has many branches.

And yes, it does not have to be hipster marketing divisions of giant companies cutting theses non-traditional deals; technically a "non-traditional" deal is simply an adeptly negotiated deal between any two parties where a variety of rights and services are exchanged that include music and music-related products. One that differs from the traditional model. Could be a multinational, a Major, an apparel company, or a rich uncle.

Wait, cutting adeptly negotiated deals contemplating a variety of rights, products and services in non-traditional ways is kinda the whole point of our new business right? Correct. The future of our business is most assuredly one in which traditional labels and third parties evolve to meet the demands of artists and their fans. But there is no blueprint here yet; for now it's just a handful smart, forward thinkers making savvy deals.

This is not theory for me, at 3QTR our entire focus is to create, adapt, and execute against ideas that have the same amount of creative energy from a business perspective as our artists do with their art. Although I will admit honestly that terms like "smart," "forward thinking," and "savvy" are a bit loose when applied to us. Likely depends on whether you are working with us to re-up a Major deal, help you develop our own branded business, make records with an indie, mailing t-shirts from USPS, owning equity in one of our companies or are dropping free songs optimized for phones on our technology platform. And, maybe more importantly, your opinion probably has a lot to do with whether or not you made any money with us.

See we dabble, iterate, and progress the business model much like our artists do songs. This is the point of entrepreneurship at any level. We run the spectrum at 3QTR—progressive, traditional, successes, failures—because while my PowerPoint deck when I launched the company was shiny utopian dreamscape, unfortunately our business operates in the real music world. Just like you.

In the real music world, you don't get to eat just because you understand that the industry is outdated and needs to change.

In the real music world you don't get to eat just because you have well articulated theories on how the business will, is likely to, or should, change.

In the real music world you get to eat by playing shows and selling as many albums and t-shirts as the market allows because it hurts just as much to not eat as it does not to make music.

This is not theory. This is killing what you eat. This is being banned from a country for your art. This is six months in jail cuz you can't afford the $1,500 in bail and fees. This is a trial gym membership so you can shower while you live in your car. This is collapsing on the stairs cuz you can't pay child care. This is not physically being able to finish the song without crying in a shed in Joshua Tree while the tin air vent and idle tape machine hum to match the depressive trance you've fallen back in. This is trying to give your all on stage and trying not to take your own life with your own prescriptions. So spare me the fucking lectures and media articles on what artists should and shouldn't be doing, how good or bad labels *really* are, how lucky artists *really* are, when you don't have to live in the real music world.

So yes, I can bag on corporate third parties, hipster Indies and Hollywood machine Majors, but I also recognize and appreciate the effort they are giving as its gonna take a concerted effort by all of us to fail at enough ideas to get to the ones that work. The more believers we can get, the more innovators we can foster, the quicker we can change things, but it doesn't change what's happening right now in real music world.

In the real music world you cut shitty Major deals because you choose dreams over quitting.

In the real music world you cut shitty indie deals because they're they only ones offering to help.

In the real music world you go DIY because no one believes in you.

In the real music world you compromise with third parties because you need a new laptop and socks.

In the real music world you go get it done cuz its music or nothing.

Ok, word, we made some music and put it out, lets go play.

THERE AIN'T NO GLAMOUR ON THE ROAD

We were up front by the driver, lined up: the band, a few friends, tour manager, merch kid, weed guy, barber, quiet, but for the engine, low growl, red light soaking us all like paratroopers before a bomb-bay door. A few of the guys are trying to make sense of the homemade banners, squinting to read scrawled text thorough tinted windows. Night. Another town, same town, all we know is the band name that's on the marquee matched the one tattooed on our legs. A now distinctly recognizable muffling of shrieks begins. The crowd over-runs the gate. New plan. Where are the cops anyway? We are getting big, but we aren't that big yet. Cops don't come until after their kids respond with your name to the refrain "what in the hell kinda noise are you listening to in there?!" We are on our own. So our security goes first. Carve a lane though the crowd. Lineman. Like he was in high school. When he met the band. Before the song went. Exploded. Before the video followed. Stratospheric. Before the deal signed, before the rush of crowds, before the buses, before the crowds with signs rushing buses that twelve dudes have been in for weeks, eating, drinking, laughing, puking, sleeping, fucking, smoking, not shitting. (Seriously, no shitting in the tour bus, that's tour rule one—if you take only one thing from this book take this.) Glamour life. All day drives that make your body shake as the diesel chem-trail hovers over you like swap fog in a dead breeze. Fuck I need off this bus. Fuck I hate this part. First time it's an adrenaline junkies dream, duck your head and charge a crowd that wants to tear you apart with an ecstatic fervor reserved for Saharan watering hole attendants. But again, these fervors are not for me. It's a Mad Max movie style run and I am one of those expendable extras who best case has the honor of being impaled before being run over on the way to Thunderdome. Red light up, we all breath heavy, collectively. Green light pings as the driver cranks the door handle, street light pours in, scream frequency hits ludicrous mode, here they come, here we go.

Touring is en vogue. Whether it is a passionate set of moments for you to express your art or a necessary evil for promotion of your album. Whether its a tech-apologists naive recommendation on how an artist "should make their money" or a corporate executive who paid to have their logo over the stage thinking they also bought the right to come hang in your backstage area and get selfies for their "kids" (you don't see me and my bands coming into your boardroom, eating free snacks and water and snapping pics - we are working here people). Point is everybody is trying to be on the road.

Why?

Well, most people believe the following to be true:

1) Touring is fun.
2) Touring is easy.
3) Touring makes you rich.

4) You are lucky.

Now this belief is held by one type of person:

1) Someone who has never been on tour.

On the surface this appears to be a fair assessment. The only time you go to shows, barring some sort of bad date, bad trip, excessive intoxicant ingestion, you are having a phenomenal time. It is entertainment after all. And the only show depictions are the glossy, well-cut, well-edited footage shared after it has been approved by a publication and/or by the artist themselves. And/or the photos and videos your friends send you that they have curated to promote their own personal awesomeness. Barring a few purposefully dark investigative documentaries, we tend to show only the good stuff and even those with the bad stuff like substance abuse and death still hold a whale's gulp of glamour and wouldn't stop most of us from hopping on the next bus through town with our favorite band.

But the key word here is "entertainment."

An artist may be a CEO of their business, but they are an entertainer of people. That's why it's called entertainment. That's why they are called shows. That's why they occur on stages. That's why there are stage managers and lighting techs and rehearsals and rehearsals and rehearsals and rehearsals and rehearsals. And rehearsals. You even say to your friends "are you going to the *show*?" "How was the *show*?" "Oh my god you missed the *show*, it was the best *show* ever!" Yet no matter how many times we say it, we don't seem to acknowledge that it is a *show* and thus... wait for it... not real life.

That is correct folks, a *show* is not the same thing as real life.

I know, I know, "but what about [insert your favorite acoustic guitar clad virtuoso, piano songstress, sit-on-a-stool-and-dim-the-lights-squinty- troubadour-dude here]?" Unless that person spontaneously started singing and playing with no intention of anyone watching while on the way to their day job, it's a show.

If she is wearing a red sequin gown leaning on a guy in a tuxedo playing a piano on a stage with a spotlight on her in an otherwise dark room surrounded by silent people who paid money to be there at the exact date and time she said she was going to be there with the intention of performing, then that is a show.

This is the touring business, *show* business.

Another Airaudi paradox shall we? Or this one is more of a Law, we can call this one Airaudi's Law of Performance Dynamics.

Airaudi's Law of Performance Dynamics: A performer's mastery of a difficult task is inversely proportional to how difficult that task appears to the observer.

See, great shows need great performers. The mark of great performance is to make the impossible look and feel as if it's easy, natural, fun. So a great performer makes an audience feel that they are having fun *with* you, feeling as if they too were a participant in the experience. And so when you do that, and by that I mean excel at your craft, and by excel at you craft I mean engage the audience in a way

124

where they are having fun with you, then you are giving the audience all the more reason to think it is all fun. And for them it is. For you to excel to that level and then sustain it night after night is not. It's work.

Now people, can you have fun at work? Yes. Are some jobs more fun than others? Yes. Does touring have moments of fun that are far superior to other work forms of fun? Hell yes. Should you make generalized assumptions about someone's vocation based on zero real world knowledge and a fantasy you have playing in your head? Hell no.

Being excellent at your job to the extent it earns you a position to do what you love is not "fun" it is a relentless lifetime commitment to making your own luck. Pick a sector.

But you get rich right?

It is true that the fees for show performances are increasing as the money in traditional recording contracts, as discussed, shrinks. Thus it is only natural for more artists to tour and/or want to tour more, believing that is where the money is. Thus more often than not artists forget the basic principle that it is a *show*. And putting on a great show is a skill. It is different skill then writing great songs, which is a different skill then making great records, which is a different skill then operating a great music company. And I know at the beginning it doesn't feel like it. In the early days you are just being you, you are winging it and people are showing up, you don't have lights and techs and choreographers, so why would you need them for a great show?

Because in the early days you are the show. You are new, undiscovered, amateur, on-the-verge. The lack of polish, the mistakes, the not-so-dialed routine, the amp blowing out, forgetting a few words, the DJ playing the wrong song, these things collectively are the show! These are the things that make you, a new artist, so exciting. It is as much peep-show as show, a secret look behind the curtain and into the process, into possibility wherein the audience now feels like they are part of the journey. And this is a critical step as these attendees will become your core fans, they will begin to evangelize for you, fight for you as you work towards world domination (they will leave you when you get half way there you sell out, but don't worry, they will be back later telling everyone about the early shows and how great the first album is). And I know you are not doing this on purpose, you are not putting on a less-than-great show because you are strategically trying to amass a core audience, I am just letting you know what is actually happening in the early arc of your touring career.

And again, you can't skip steps. Even when you don't realize exactly what step you are on. Miss this one and no core. No core, no long-term sustainability. So don't wait for the show to be great, go make it great.

These early days are the best times, in my opinion, and why I will always work with up-and-coming artists in some capacity. A frenetic and magically brief period when all the years of work and prep, all the sacrifice and self-doubt, have converged to place you rattling on the launch pad; consumed by the smoke and the fire to the point where each breath is heavy with the knowledge that at any second you will suffocate, explode or shoot into the stratosphere. There is no point at which you feel more alive.

And don't worry if you throw up; when you go up, you pull some serious G's.

Now that's a fuckin' show.

But then the smoke and shock settles. And whether you made it to the moon, an uncharted galaxy or the Toledo Country Fair, the initial show is over and now you need to be entertaining. Let us agree this is again a wildly subjective term, "entertaining," but what is not subjective is whether or not a lot of people chose to see you perform.

THE ENTERTAINER

For some a show is to sit at the piano and sing, strum that guitar, and tell stories. For others it's getting a few of their closest friends together, three in a tight set or fifty launching into a three-hour jam session. Still others launch pyrotechnics and raid their mom's make up drawer. You can make people dance or cry or be silent. Make people laugh and kiss the one they came with. Make people bounce and kiss the one they just met. It all good, there's no correct way to do it other than to make it compelling to group of people large enough that the amount of money they leave at the door minus the fees of operating that door is enough to cover your gas, hamburgers, and drum heads.

Show business.

There's that tricky word again, business. You are CEO, but now you just need to be the CE, chief entertainer. CE no O. And all of this sounds so great right, except for the pesky part where you need to make money.

So what about that money? Everyone is saying touring is where the money is, so where's the money?

Good question.

It is important to note that, for artists, the money from the music business is not growing. Yes, the touring industry is growing, yes it feels like more money is coming in, but of it is not. Core music money merely shifted from one source, records, to alternative music consumption sources, live shows, exclusive merch, etc. (There is an area where music is driving new and real revenue, we will get to that.) As touched on previously, spare music-related cash coupled with the public's increased desire for "experiences" and you get more people going to / paying for live shows. Now add to that social media platforms that allow you to you broadcast your personal experience so that digital acquaintances can be made envious by thinking you are having a great experience and you have a massive increase in live show attendance.

So the touring pie may inflate due to consumers assigning greater value to and thus shifting their wallets from music goods to music experiences, but the music business overall, whether revenue derived from product or experience, is not growing.

Screw this marco market economics mumbo jumbo man, what about my slice?!?!?

The artist cut? Well, that is sure as hell not growing because while the promoters are busy upselling parking and popcorn and data and streaming rights, you are still just getting a fee. Sure that fee may net you are extra 10 percent more than it used to, but it doesn't offset the 80 percent decrease in your recorded music income. And remember, each of the recorded music dollars that finds its way into your pocket is yours to keep; every dollar earned on the road comes with the sustained costs of staying out on the road (more on that in a moment).

Further, this inflated pie, as with any good bloating, is happening mostly to old people and the rich 1 percent. Pop superstars and legacy bands with fans that now have disposable incomes and dusty CD collections are flocking in droves to see their favorite nostalgia band or take the kids to the pop artist of the month or, as referenced earlier, playing dress up via gentrification enabled hipster boutique and popping adult candy at whatever random festival their daughter and her friends loved five years ago.

Now this is ALL good. I do not judge musical tastes (nor ones recreational pharmaceutical practices). So like what you like, but, much like any other product, people tend to like the same stuff, thus that stuff that is liked gets liked more and more and becomes stuff that is liked by lots of people and thus becomes popular (or what I like to call The Pop 1 Percent). Thus we get the perpetuation of a small subset of liked artists i.e., the most popular artists. This is also all good, it's how "breaking" into the masses works, but practically it means that those already liked get more liked. Or, as my favorite Nobel laureate economics professor puts it, the rich getting richer. Not a conspiracy, not impartiality, just another tenet, however beloved or objectionable, of our blessed capitalism.

My point is touring income at the artist level, your level, is complimentary, not substitutional, income.

I am going to repeat and dive in briefly here for the technology apologists who have the continued audacity to tell artists how they should operate their businesses, namely "artists should go make money touring." Un-namely, so technology companies can continue reaping the profits generated by your digital content byproduct. Nothing to see here folks! Just trillions of views, likes, clicks, streams and $100B plus in technology company valuations that house and broadcast that content! I digress.

The punchline on touring income is it's the same as earning it in other aspects of the business. If you can scale your business to reach millions of fans, then you will also be on TV and in magazines, invited to "it" events to be photographed and broadcast via socials and have millions of followers – and then you can make money on live shows too. The same way you will be making money selling records, t-shirts, stickers, etc. And vice versa.

Touring doesn't make you rich, it is an additional profit stream available to artists who have worked hard to get a significantly large physical fan base. ("Physical" because you can have a large digital following, but no one that cares to physically show up to see you per form.) Only after you have this large physical fan base can you then decide if you want to focus on live performances and grow that line of business. And then there is the issue is opportunity cost i.e., what else are you giving up in order to put on shows. Seems like another obvious point but there is a reason it has an official name, "opportunity cost", most people don't think about it, but for touring it is of paramount concern. Why? Putting on a tour takes a ton of dedicated time and focus—coming up with creative, hiring team, rehearsing, travel, shows, you can be gone for months (years)–so you can't just think about what you are earning from tour, but what are you *not* earning cuz you are on tour (thus have no time to make new music, do photoshoots, star in movies, whatever).

Besides, when people say "artists make money touring" and thus "artists should *just* tour" it is a bit like saying basketball players make money playing in professional games so basketball players should *just* join the NBA.

And notice I said "profit" stream. The revenue stream is open to anyone with a tune, but profitability is another matter. Starting to notice a theme? Any artist can get in their moms car and book some shows the same way any artist can upload a song to the internet. That's not making profit and that's sure as hell not making a living.

So why can't we all make a living from touring?

TOURING ECONOMICS, LOGISTICS AND... ZZZZZZ... HUH, WHAT, WAIT, SORRY, I FEEL ASLEEP IN THE MIDDLE OF THE TITLE

If people value experiences, socials are driving demand, and money is pouring, shifting, bloating, whatever into the live performance space than why can't we all eat off the touring money?

Well, besides the fact that no one knows who you are in the beginning, all those thousands of digital followers you are amassing do not translate to ticket sales (how many of your followers, even if they all do want to spend money on your show, are in Cleveland this Wednesday at 11p.m.?), and touring is expensive.

But let's say can you get a few folks out to see you, lets look at what you will need, at a base level:

Base Level Touring Necessity List
- Gear
- Transit (car, tolls, parking, oil, brake job, subway pass, etc.)
- Food
- Hotels

But then you have to perform too so you can't do everything that needs to be done on the road yourself and do it day after day after day. I mean you can, if you have a terrible show and no one wants to see you, but then, see, you can't tour.

Base Level Touring Things-You-Need-To-Do List

- Book shows
- Get to shows
- Load-in (i.e., pack all the gear into the venue)
- Sound check, line check (i.e., test your noise making)
- Play the show
- Load-out (i.e., pack all the gear out of the venue)
- Settle the show (i.e., get paid)

So lets assume you knocked out the basics above a few times and now people want to see you on more than one occasion somewhere within driving distance of your home. Now what? You got some willing buyers, some willing players and lets assume you have some usable gear since you somehow made some music that attracted said buyers. So now we have what appears to be a burgeoning touring business.

Lets break it down a bit.

And lets assume you have a booking agent, i.e., someone whose job it is to liaise with venues and promoters and get you on a stage to perform your music. BTW, a booking agent is worth every penny. And that penny is worth 10 percent off the top, that's the standard fee. Find a great one, I am telling you. I have had great and they fight and fight and are pivotal in your growth. I have had bad and never been berated worse in my life then when I told them we were leaving to find a new agent. Worth every insult I took.

And why am I assuming you have one? Because otherwise you have to start this process by spending a whole host of time trying to get someone to even let you play at their venue. This is a business book, not a how-to book and, being that I am not an artist, I don't know how-to do it. Book shows. It's another one of my "simple, not easy" items.

So next stop should be a tour manager, or a "TM." The homie will do at first, but this is thankless, difficult, dirty, exhausting job so it takes a special kind of person to do it well. Much like a nuclear reactor maintenance manager they are basically paid to do a bunch of shit nobody else wants to nor knows how to and their only success metric is perfection.

The Great Tour Manager Paradox is that their job responsibilities are inversely proportional to their talent and knowledge. In the beginning they have to do everything and have no idea about anything. Anyone can get the basic idea down like renting vans, booking flights and hotels, handling merch, driving and that all sounds easy until you break it down further. You are on an insanely small, fixed budget and in a new city, likely one none of you have ever been to before, everyday. TM has to calculate drive times, source hotels, ones that you can afford, have a credit card, have enough room on that credit card to book all these rooms then get everyone in and out of these hotels and cars at exactly the right time. Gear has to be in proper shape, fit in whatever vehicle they have determined falls within the budget and remain in proper shape. Then merch has to be made, shipped, hauled, setup, broke down and most critically, accounted for, i.e., counted in, counted out, you need proper change, are you taking credit cards? Now you need a chip reader and an iPad, and that iPad

134

needs a case, and you need to charge that iPad. Cool, but the TM has been in a van all day, driving in the rain on three hours sleep and they were the one responsible for getting everyone up early, checking out, loading up the car, grabbing some coffees and rolling papers cuz everyone else is going to want to smoke in the nonsmoking passenger van that they were able to book over the phone because they told the nice lady y'all were a "church group." Someone's gotta pee, someone's sick, someone's phone is dead, there's no windshield wiper fluid, and you left the drum key at the last venue. Etc.

And everyone is living it up, especially on these early tours, but TM has to be sober because they are responsible for advancing the shows, getting to the shows, managing the shows, settling with the venue after the shows a.k.a., getting the money and getting out of that shit hole in time to make Albuquerque.

Some key basic terms:

Advancing is coordinating everything about the show day with those putting on the show because while the show may start at 9 p.m., doors open at 7 p.m., so you have to be done with soundcheck at 6p.m., but no, you are just the opening band so IF they even let you soundcheck, yours is at 3:30pm. Either way that means you gotta have all that gear set up on stage by 2 p.m., which means you are loading in by 1 p.m. and wait, how far away was the city you played in last night? How far is the city you play in tomorrow?

Sound check vs. line check vs. hahaha...ha?

Soundcheck is when you get to set up you gear, run through a song to two and dial in the sound that both you hear on stage and the audience hears off stage with the team in charge of sound at the venue before the audience enters. (Eventually you will have your own sound person, oh that's the best, not yet though, you can barely afford to get to the show yourself, you are lightyears from traveling an extra person you have to pay a salary + travel + food + lodging, we will get into this soon.)

Line check is when the gear is all mic'd up for you and run through a quick test run right before you start your set, i.e., with the audience staring at you like a dope.

Hahaha...ha is the response you get in the early days from the sound guy when you ask when your soundcheck is. Get used to it. And good luck grabbing new fans when you sound like shit, rookie! No worries, nobody will show up that early to watch you anyway.

Settling is getting the money. Easy enough but these contracts are not. Flat money for opening is easy, but it's often a formula—promoter fees, venue fees (venues often take a piece of merch too, get out that spreadsheet and cash box, these dudes are not shy about accepting crumpled up bills) percentage of door, overages, etc. And this is your money, your livelihood, make-or-break your tight budget so it better all be right and it's 2 a.m. and you gotta sleep a few hours before you drive again.

And just when you are getting the hang of it, wham! Some success!

So now for the tricky part—you trying to scale another music business. (Go CE/O!)

So the audience grows and now the venues grow and thus the team must grow correspondingly. Three or four people in a shitty van will need to become seven or eight in a sprinter van and you will need a driver, a merch person, a sound engineer. Oh and its a "show" remember, so you need some combination of lights, set design, choreography, which means people to maintain those lights, set up the set, etc. And all of this sounds silly to the struggling rapper or punk band when a few kids come get drunk and shell out $5 at the local spot and you feel like a rock star, but, as described, audiences, at some point, expect a show, pay for a show and thus must be given a great fucking show.

So the TM now does not and cannot perform all of these functions personally, but now they must coordinate and oversee it all. The good news is the best way to understand someone's job is to do it and a young TM does nothing but do everyone's job that you can't afford to bring on the road. A good one anyway. So you and the TM must find great people, because this work is hard work and not many people have the temperament, the stamina, the attention to detail, smarts, fitness, thick skin, arrogance, stomach and general steel constitution it takes to go out night after night, town after town, sick, sober, drunk, hungry, depressed, lonely, isolated, exhausted and dive deep to find the will to put on a fake smile and a real show at the level of perfection that both artist and fan will hold you to.

Pause and salute the true TMs for a second, they are worth their weight in gold.

Great artists understand this. Great artists want this. Not just for the pageantry of show, but for a base level of consistent amazingness. And great sound. This is a music show remember? No level of ceremony can gloss over shit sound. Great sound can quell any sub-par theatrics. So after a great TM, get you a great FOH.

The FOH, a.k.a., front of house, a.k.a., "sound person," is the most critical person in your life once you arrive at the venue. Many a TM double as FOH early days, the great ones anyway, but as you scale this becomes a singular, indispensable position. We won't spend a ton of time here as the rationale is glaringly obvious, but for whatever reason many artists overlook it. You are a musician playing music at a show people came to use their ears to listen to; if it doesn't sound good there is no point to the rest of your pomp. Every venue has a different mixing board, room shape, stage shape, speaker system, wiring, house gear, etc. Someone needs to bring a level of consistency to the sound of your show every night, whatever the room. Again here, for the FOH, success is measured by two criteria: perfect or not.

Another pause and salute, to the great FOH!

The trend continues CEO, you need more greatness from more great people around you to grow your business in this new vertical i.e., your live entertainment division i.e., selling tickets. As you rise so will the bar for your definition of great. At the same time the audience will now be shifting from hardcore fans to the passive masses. See the percentage of core fans in attendance is inversely proportional to show quality standards. In the early days your shows are sparsely attended, but all are faithful, they love you. A bad show is just part of the charm as described. In the later days those core fans get drowned out by new fans, passive fans, even those that maybe feigning interest just to get to spend time with some other people going to the show for their own reasons. However worthy or unworthy, these folks always demand a great show.

Whatever the reason for attending, at whatever level, there are too many options and distractions in this world for somebody to work all week, scrimp and save, choose to spend one of their precious nights off only to watch you prance around alone with a mic, in poor lighting, with blown out low end and shit quality recoded backing vocals that combine to strain ears and patience because you chose to save some money.

Respect the people.

Respect the people and they will respect you back. They will respect you back by coming back with friends, singing your songs, buying a shirt and asking you to sign it. They will do this while you are respecting your fans even more by going out to the merch booth after your show to thank people for coming out even though you feel like you could die or at least sleep and you still have to load out and drive through the night to make Austin.

And respect costs money. Cuz great people cost money. Vans cost money, tour buses cost more. Flights and hotels and per diems for a traveling party of five to ten people is expensive as shit. Lets list out typical expenses:

Average Touring Expense List
- 4 rooms per night minimum for 8 people
- 8 Flights and/or train tickets for each longer leg
- Production expenses
- Band salary, per member, per show
- Band PD, per member, daily (PD = per diem, like a daily allowance for food)
- TM salary + PD, daily
- FOH salary + PD daily
- Tech salary + PD daily
- Merch salary + PD, daily
- Driver salary + PD, daily
- Van/bus/car service
- Gear/equipment
- Replacement gear/equipment
- Gas, tolls, parking, parking tickets (always), cabs, oil changes, etc.
- Bag fees
- Insurance*

* Yes, there is such thing as band insurance. You can play dumb for a while, we all do and honestly you can't really afford to do it any other way, but having been on the business end of the lawsuit baton, I can assure you this is key as soon as anyone starts to think you have money. And that point is well before you actually do have money as we have addressed everyone thinks touring artists are rich. And for you punk-ethos fuck-the-man, mosh pit, stage dive band who think your craziness has no cost think again; insurance is literally where

the man is gonna get you.

And that's an average crew. With no surprises. The bigger the crew, the better the gear, the greater the show, the longer the run the more money it costs. And the increased likelihood of surprises. So yes your guarantees are going up every night, but your costs are rising proportionally, well, typically disproportionally faster—why? Because you have to keep putting on greater and greater shows to build your audience, and that costs more money.

You are deficit funding your business (the entrepreneurship continues).

And you physically can't play every night. You need to rest and travel and it all has to "route" properly, meaning there has to be a show to play the night after your last show within a reasonable distance of the one you just played. And you can't do that for 30 days in a row, so maybe you are squeezing 20 shows into those 30 days. In business speak that is 20 revenue-earning days over 30 cost days. Great agents will help with this.

Note: If you do it yourself you are guaranteed to overestimate your stamina. The road is unforgivingly hard. I once meet an artist who played 70 shows in 90 days in 17 countries. I signed him immediately.

And you only see approximately 60 percent of that money. (Remeber agents, managers, business managers, lawyers all commission here–label too if you signed a 360, don't sign a 360.)

So income is increasing costs that are increasing, when so will it reach equilibrium? Or better yet, when do fee increases begin to outpace the expense required to provide great shows? Now this can vary on the extremes of the spectrum (solo DJ with a backpack or 22-piece jazz ensemble), but the ballpark number for a typical singer and/or band is around $10,000 per show.

Yes, $10,000.

There are not a lot of people averaging $10,000 plus a night. And when you make $10,000 a night, you are not rich. You are breaking even. Now, I have refrained from the math, but you gotta get deeper into the weeds if you are gonna survive tour. Besides I assume you can breakdown ounces to dollars so you will be fine here.

Let's just add some math from my above list. How much you think it costs to fly 8 people to/from Europe and travel for a month? If you are paying on average of $150/night for a room and 5 rooms that's $750/night + tax and fees call it $1k for 30 nights that's $30,000 in hotels. Before the exchange rate. Just hotels. Cheap hotels with half the crew sharing a room. You need to book 8 economy flights to and from and one or two while you are over there, probably another $20k. Lets use $10k per show on 20 shows so you are in grossing $200k, call it $180k after foreign tax withholding and call it $100k after fees (agent, lawyers, etc.) so you whacking 50 percent off the top before you even start the tour and we just said there's $50k in hotels and flights so you got $50k left and you haven't left your house.

And lets be honest, if you are making $10k a night / $200k all-in for a tour your team is not all sharing shitty hotel rooms. Nor are great TMs gonna bunk up just to save you cash, plus they need space to do work; in fact good ones will run you minimum $500/day so there's another minimum $15k off the top.

And for the hold out rappers and 2-piece punk bands that make $250 a night + free beer saying my $10k/night number is crazy, let's not forget we just covered the topic of what it means to put on a "show." By the time to are commanding $10k fees the people paying you and the people watching you are going to need more than just you and the homie playing tracks off a laptop and/or thrashing your body all over stage. Not if you want to be asked back and certainly not if you hope to reach and sustain greatness. Remember, in this complex media world with people seeking "experiences," that is what you need to provide.

The one exception here might be club DJs. These kids make mad money to stand in front of a computer and bounce up in down in a club. Now I am not saying "stand" in a derogatory manner. Far from it. Before we chide the DJs as doing nothing and pressing buttons, lets take a step back and understand how tour fees are calculated. Tour fees are calculated by how many people you get to come out to the venue. There are various ways to get people out and you did it, so did the DJ, by years and years of scaling your music and fan base. Fees may technically be for the evening, but what you are truly being paid for is the years and years of work it took to build your busineses and brand to the point where it is not only a good decision, but a highly profitable one for someone to pay you to come make some noise. And if they are paying you to stand on a stage and play music off a computer, then you for sure spent some serious time off stage building an audience.

As I have said before with DJs, if that sounds like "doing nothing" then you should do it. And simple not easy doesn't even apply here, because the technical skill, music knowledge, and brand development a successful DJ must possess is not simple or easy. Nor is scaling it for 10 years in an industry that has consistently failed to respect your art as art.

Good work if you can get it. DJ go ahead and get it.

(Note to self: Register, trademark, my new DJ name "DJ Go-Ahead-And-Get-It.")

ADDITIONAL COSTS

This is work. This is a business. This is long days under adverse conditions pumping all your blood and sweat into the show and all your show cash back into the business. This is entrepreneurship. But at least we, non-artist, entrepreneurs get to curl up fetal position and cry in the privacy of our own shower floors when it's just too much to bear. We fake it and smile to our partners and our friends, but you, artist, have to face the camera. You have to get on that stage, do interviews and talk about how great it feels, how wonderful it all is. You have to maintain the facade in person, digitally, in the press.

And don't you dare let your guard down for a second. Don't you dare do it with an ounce of ingratitude or a hint of perceived ungraciousness or you will be lambasted for it. Not because the press and general public are assholes, but because they don't understand, they can't understand what you are enduring by offering up your soul in the decades long marathon that is a successful touring career. They just want a quick pic and pithy soundbite for their blog. All good. That's their business.

Nobody will understand. Nobody will know.

Nobody will appreciate how hard it is, how hard you will have to be working to earn the mere opportunity to lose money touring. (Make money? That's the top 5 percent and 20 percent of that is the Pop 1 percent.) In fact, worse, they will believe the exact opposite, that you are lucky. And to be fair, you asked for this job and its likely way better than their job so even though they are wrong in their assumptions of your financial and lifestyle largess, they are still correct in that as measured by the awesomeness ratio "your job to their job" likely tilts solidly in your direction. And you can't blame them for not being understanding or sympathetic because no one can truly understand another person's life, certainly one as unique as an artist's. On top of that your life is now being designed, for marketing and promotional purposes, to look as amazing as possible. Of course they give no fucks for you, you are a big rich rock star! Unfortunately for you, your right to a non-intrusive "normal" life was stripped from you unknowingly when you asked people to listen and they agreed.

That said, I wouldn't trade the experience for the world. Everything worth anything in life is hard fucking work. There ain't glamour on the road, cuz there ain't glamour in work. The glamour is in the glory. But all glory is fleeting. So enjoy it in the pockets and pauses, stay in those beautiful moments a bit longer when you recognize they are happening and learn to love the road as that's where you will live as you scale your business.

Think back to my 30 day tour example for a second—that's 20 shows with an average set time (time on stage) of hour and change so you are playing maybe 25 hours of live music over that period. Minus the 200 hours of sleep and naps that mean 95 percent of your waking hours are spent OFF the stage. And how much of that 5 percent do you think will be great? Not by fan standards, but by your meticulous, remorseless, self-critique? Remember to keep the fans happy, but keep yourself happy too. And don't be too hard on yourself. That's the business.

One day on such a business trip I woke up in the den of some rented desert house.

The owner came back to check his email at 6 a.m. He said he thought no one would be up. I said I thought we paid for a house. He said he would only be a moment and clacked away at the keys as I lay on a stone floor beneath him in a pile of blankets and cushions like I lost a grappling fight with a grandma loveseat. I coughed uncontrollably. Any thicker a coat of smoke resin and beer and you could not have legally called it air. It was aquarium-esque. The owner could not have been pleased. Maybe that's what he was emailing about. But when you price-gouge rent your house last minute to a band and their friends on their first major festival date you are gonna earn that money, Mr. Landlord.

I strolled into the main house. The last of the guys had just gone to sleep. Lobby Call i.e., the exact time we are all required to convenne in the lobby to meet our transportation, in this case it was a "Drive-way" Call, was not for 4 hours. Our landlord having finally depart-ed, I surveyed the scene. Beer and medical weed bottles. Cereal and pizza boxes. Cigarette and milk cartons. Hot Pockets and Arizona Ice Teas. Two guys on the couch, peacefully siesta'd, fully clothed. One guy fast asleep in the small bedroom off the kitchen with a glass of water and a tea on the nightstand. Another with no clothes and company. Guys on the floor, girls curled up in chairs, a couple pass me on their way out the door with what I now recognize as a "stan-dard" downward glance and half smile comprised of equal parts guilt, embarrassment, and joy. Combing Instagram to fill in the gaps in the evening. I find a hot pot of coffee on in kitchen, back between a burnt towel and half bag of sugar. The other half on the floor like snowman guts. I pour a cup, smell it, cuz you never know, step over a few folks and out the siding glass doors to the pool.

The sun already rallying against the crispness of the desert night. My lone animate band member nods and exhales a long white streak of medical grade cannibus. Anxiety. At least that's the story he told the "doctor" in the emerald bikini top and green and white American flag bandana. And stethoscope. On roller skates. When he got his medical card in that bastion of advanced healthcare and my home of Venice Beach. He wasn't lying. About the anxiety. And in fairness the weed did help although the 6:30 a.m. variety was probably not advisable especially given the throat issues from singing night after night on the road. He told me that's when it's the worst. The anxiety. The mornings. You spend your whole day getting accustomed to it. Working through it. Getting over it just enough to give a great show. Being ok with accolades after. When you feel in your heart you were terrible. But your therapist said that's not your heart, it's your head, and not really even your head, but some amino acid chain therein being built, pumped and flooded into your system, but you fail to see a difference cuz you are sweaty and emotionally spent and everyone else is smiling and drinking and smoking and acting like it was them who jut splayed their chest open on stage and display their heart for the amusement of strangers. In the morning you gotta start the cycle all again, cuz this when you remember that you are an imposter.

You are a fake.

In reality you are just a messed up kid who loves art and sound and wants to share it. And now in doing so is being forced to make it all up as you go along. You had a hard enough time fitting in in high school and now you have to smile for different cameras as you sing the same songs, tell the same stories, trying your best to be that person they all envision in their heads. If you don't smile and sign you are an asshole. If you would like to eat your dinner in peace you are ungrateful. If you don't meet the personal expectations of 100 percent of the people you meet 100 percent of the time you are a conceited jerk to someone. If you want to keep sound checking until its sounds perfect, because, umm, sound is the fucking business you're in, then you are a prima donna. If you hold out for the money you think you are worth, you are greedy. If you disagree with what has been done traditionally, you are a "kid" who doesn't "get it." And even if you could get past all that, it's a fee-for-performance business on which fees are taken, so if you want to take a night off that means everyone around you is taking the night of i.e., not working i.e., not making money.

Heavy.

My friend inhales and offers it to me even though he knows I don't smoke. I decline and say thank you; I always appreciate the gesture. When you are on the road it's the little shared kindnesses that get you through. Someone brings you a water. Unloads your bag. Let's you have the top bunk. Passes the blunt.

He says he made coffee. I nod and lift the mug in my hand. He nods and say's he's not sure he can do the show today. Says he has been up for hours. Lost his medication, the non-green-bikini-prescribed one. I say don't worry you'll be great. He says he is not sure. He is being honest. I am not. The truth on the road is that despite the monotony everyday is a new start. New town, new food, new state of mind. Planes and vans, ups and downs, tears and laughter, fist fights and hallucinations. It's dirty, long, exhausting, thankless, expensive and you gotta maintain everybody else's preconception that you are the luckiest person in the world. And maybe you are. Maybe this is what luck feels like. But you are still at work. And this is still a job. And only the greats get that, work like that, and survive like that. For a time.

By the time my caffeine fix kicks in the sun is up and searing the landscape. We both get up and look out over the immaculately manicured garden and pool. "Let's swim," he says. "Do we have time?"

I ask. "Fuck it, backlining and line check right? We can roll right up and play."

"So you are gonna play the show then?" I say smiling.

He returns the wide, school-boy mid-prank grin that makes the fans melt. "Fuck you."

We swim.

Mainstage at 4 p.m.

III. DO'S, DON'TS, ~~DEPRESSION~~, DESTINY

BRANDS ON BRANDS ON BRANDS

I found and co-managed a crew whose early work, like that of any great artistic outcast kids, did a fantastic job of scaring the beejezzus out of everyday people. Eating roaches, pulling out fingernails and teeth, performing in ski masks, diving off 20 foot speakers, jumping on network televisions hosts backs, on stage water fights (with the water still in the bottle), we introduced mosh pits to young rap fans and major labels to the next IDGAF generation.

We used all of this to build a brand.

Notice I said "build." You build brands. They do not just spontaneously appear as plenty of music business folks like to believe now that it's an industry buzzword. Brands aren't leprechauns, they don't show up with a pot of gold because you got a dope green outfit and people chasing you.

For artists, brand is often misconstrued as a bad word, a corporate exploitation that detracts from the music. But remember our Zen lessons, it is not about the music, it is about the music. An artist brand is just the halo created around when your music mixes with oxygen and irresistibility. Deny it and they will just paint it on you later.

For the business folks, "brand" is a loose term. I have heard it used as a noun "we need to make a brand!"; as a verb "we need to brand!"; as an adjective "we need brand people!"; as a financing vehicle "we need money from brands!"; and generally as a place holder to sound

152

as if you are laying out a smart strategic solution to all your music business woes in a single concise action plan, "we need to be a brand!" The trouble with all this *needing* is that first thing everyone *needs* to do is understand what they are talking about.

Before we get into definitions, lets talk about what a brand is not.

A brand is not a logo.
A brand is not art on a shirt.
A brand is not a "movement."
A brand is not an artist who is a celebrity.
A brand is not an artist who has made lots of sales.
Branding is not marketing.

It is important to note however, that included in the above list are componnents of what will ultimately become your overall brand should you be lucky enough to build one.

So what then are we talking about?

Simply, a brand is an identity people immediately recognize as unique and having real value.

The key here is "real value." To be a brand, and the whole point in building a brand, is to advantage yourself in the market. Brands have meaning to consumers and this meaning allows you to command a higher price for your goods (stuff) relative to competitors goods (other stuff). Macs cost substantially more then PCs for instance. Now because the meaning conveyed by a brand extends more broadly then any specific good (stuff) or service (doing stuff) this gives you the opportunity to expand your goods and services (stuff) into new markets/verticals. Apple computers to phones to self driving cars for instance.

Nuances and academia side, for artists, you create such an association to your name (say Dr. Dre) so that when you have a non-recorded-music product or service in the market (say headphones), fans/consumers, have an immediate idea of what they are getting (say Grammy award-winning, street shattering, iconic, bass rich sound) simply by seeing your name attached to them.

And this is not a new phenomenon. The greatest music brand off all time is the Grateful Dead. People literally stopped living their daily lives and started to live the Grateful Dead lifestyle 50+ years ago. Try that today. Try having music so great, a personality so charming, a way of existing so compelling that people quit their jobs and dedicate themselves to yours. And not just following you around and living out of VW busses and selling veggie burritos to teens, but living by the principles of your music. Pot brownies to tie dye to dancing bear plush toys, a music-based brand is only as powerful as the music it is rooted in.

So these band brands have always existed, they just were not typically described as such. No one was writing case studies on a Grateful Dead *brand*, it all just seemed a natural extension of their music. And it was! An artists' brand always begins as a byproduct of their everyday activities. Until recently it was exploited simply as a nice complimentary value to help sell more tickets and recorded music.

154

Eventually, artists began to have meaning beyond their music, impacting markets all around them. This halo effect we now refer to as a brand. And it can keep growing. Eventually there were "Dead Heads" (followers of the Grateful Dead lifestyle) that didn't even listen to the Grateful Dead's music. Conversely, some people became fans of the band's music only after they discovered the brand. Jerry Garcia didn't build the Dead to sell bumper stickers to trust fund college kids pretending to be hippies, but he did ensure that the trademarks and ownership allowed him to be compensated when they adopted the specific lifestyle he popularized. Again, it's not sell-out-boring-business-shit to own and be compensated of the value you build. Unfortunately for you, no longer are brands a nice ancillary halo, they are a necessity.

And yes, some artists hate the whole idea of brands, but that does not mean they don't have them. Many choose not to acknowledge or exploit the halo around them, but the point is not that they are good or bad, just that they exist. And if you don't exploit it someone else will (or already is). Nothing of value sits idle in our society for long. Paparazzi to magazine covers to critics to sweatshop knockoffs to movie characters that "bear a resemblance" to a fashion company building a look or season based on what you wear. If you move culture, people will use you to move their customers—or make your customers, theirs. I mean if you wear a jacket that is available at retail to an award show it will be sold out the next morning and the screenshots will be on the jacket makers corporate socials.

So is it "better" to own and be compensated fairly for the work you have done? Or is it better ceding it to some global advertising agency or bored, savvy kid on the internet making knock off merch? Which one is more artistic?

It doesn't matter if you are an Adele or a Jay Z.

An "Adele" meaning an uniquely exceptional talent that puts albums out every few years and doesn't have ten lines of clothing and brands because she is a "real artist" (BTW, I hate that term—a fake artist is an oxymoron). Being a "real" artist IS her brand. This is a choice. And perhaps a smart one. You can't own sneakers and fragrances and also claim to care *only* about music. If you have other businesses you obviously care about those or you would not have them. This is not good or bad, but it is defining your brand. All your non-music brands will dilute your music brand at some level. Again, this is why brand development is a strategy and skill and requires hard work and smart people to do right. It's not about the money, it's about being intensely smart about being the artist you want to be so you can 1) sustain a career in a world people don't pay for music as product and 2) justly be compensated for the actual value you are creating in the world.

A "Jay Z" on the other hand, is an uniquely exceptional talent who successfully takes the power of his reach and influence back from the third parties who were exploiting it and builds a global conglomerate. Jay is an artist who evolved to entrepreneur to business icon. He is no less of an artist because of his success in business, but his success as a businessman devalues his music brand as a result. Note, the loss of value is to the artist "brand," i.e., the halo, i.e., the perception; there is no actual decline in the actual artistry. This is just the nature

156

of our world, a person can be a great artist and great businessperson, but a brand cannot stand equally for art and commerce. You just gotta pick a spot on the spectrum where you are comfortable standing.

Lets take a look at this spectrum:

EXHIBIT 2. COMMERCE V. ART

COMMERCE	v.		ART
MACHO MAN RANDY SAVAGE*	JAY Z	ADELE	CHANTING HERMIT MONKS

* If you have not heard wrestling legend Macho Man Randy Savage's rap album please stop reading and find it immediately.

So for business folk: Educate yourself and surround yourself with people who know how to develop and manage brands. That is the world we live in. Music product is a commodity. Music is content. I don't care if you like the way that sounds or not (I don't), but it does not negate the fact that it is true and our responsibility in the serving of our clients to cultivate anything and everything that will differentiate them in the marketplace, command higher prices and diversify our product/service offerings. It's not a matter of if we *want* to be in the brand business, we are. And artists are not supposed to be good at building and managing brands, they are just good at being them. It is our job to focus on the commercial aspects of their lifestyle.

Adapt.

For artists: The key for you is to stay true to self. One of my favorite hip-hop cliches of all time is "real recognize real"—it is the perfect summation of human species innate ability to pick up on honesty. And it is the uniqueness of your art, your talent, your imperfections, your ambition, your humility, your successes and failures, and the manner in which you endure all of it that radiates a halo about you.

This will become the un-mimic-able foundation of your brand. That is why it exists whether you monetize it or not. You don't start by picking an idea, you start by being honest. Same way you don't pick a band name first, you start making coordinated sounds. Follow that with hard work and surround yourself with people who know how to grow brands and businesses from brands. You are an entrepreneur and CEO of your own company, your function day to day is to 1) make art and 2) get the people you bring on to execute against your vision.

Yes, some artists will become global stars and never be commercial brands. And that will be their brand. They will just be huge stars, sell music, and sell out stadiums. If you are one of these or work for one of these, congratulations. Don't change. Enjoy the old music business, very few of us get to.

[Deleted]

Now I had a whole long chapter here. I laid out the analysis and steps and stages of brand development, the pitfalls of overreach and the monetization mechanisms attached, but I deleted it. The truth is, the brand is the same as your music. It's you and I can't tell you how to be you. The same way you only work with great creatives to make great music, only work with great business people to build your brand. (Writing and deleting is apropos considering I had to try and fail to do this to learn the lesson.)

Ultimately, brand development is about being and staying true to yourself and your music.

ASSETS & EQUITY

Wow this chapter heading is terrible, but it's so important I couldn't leave it out. Lets just get into it, briefly.

Most people in this business spend most of their time chasing checks, but that's not a business, that's a hustle. Now you can get rich hustling checks, sure, but you'll get exhausted and slow down, and the checks will slow with it. If want to get rich, cool, put this book down and go on, but here we are talking about making your great grandkids wealthy. You can't get wealthy without equity and assets.

Brands are your foray into non-music-asset-dependent businesses, i.e., income and value that is not tied directly to your music and personal popularity at a given time. Brands are a simple way of advancing your *ownership* in the marketplace, whether by you owning the brand yourself or lending your cultural relevance to other brands/

business in exchange for equity.

And that's the holy grail of deals. Equity. But what exactly is it and how do you get it?

If you leverage your music to build your brand, your reach, and your impact to the point where other business people (outside of music) can attribute quantifiable value to *your* ability to help grow *their* business, that is when you get cut in on ownership. That is equity. That is not a check, it is ownership in the underlying business that you are helping to create. Artists do this all the time from rapping about alcohol brands to wearing shoes to carrying a handbag to frequenting a particular hotel. And you may get paid for doing these things if you reach enough people, but you won't get equity unless you first prove your brand value in the market. And "brand value" outside of music will be judged by tangible success metrics such as profit, cash, assets value, etc. This is why Coke pays you $10k to do a private branded Vitamin Water show, but they paid 50 Cent tens of millions of dollars when they bought Vitamin Water for $4B—he owned equity.

Small equity can mean big money. It also means long development time. So be patient. But be smart patient. Diversify your portfolio. No longer can you wait for publishing income to come in the mail 30 years from now. Nor do you want to be working on the glamourless road 30 years now (outside of the Vegas residency of course) to keep the income coming in. Equity is not a guaranteed byproduct of success in music. It must be built.

And when you build a portfolio of equity, you begin to create real assets.

And that's the holy grail of your career. Real, non-music-celebrity-trend based value that you own and control.

This is how you win in today's music business. When your music and team is so powerful that you have equity and assets building value for you simply as an offshoot of your day-to-day activities marketing and promoting your art e.g., you have equity in the companies that makes your favorite t-shirt and keyboard (that you wear/use on stage, in videos, etc.), you own the agricultural land that grows your brand of weed, you are on the board of the self-driving trucking company that moves your gear to shows, etc. That's how you extract the *real* value of your music in the marketplace, that is how you own the totality of your work output, that is how you maximize long term asset value for yourself and your family, that is how you have so much fucking money that you tell everyone and anyone that has a comment on your creative work what hole in which to reinsert their criticism and go make unadulterated, raw, soul devouringly beautiful acoustic reverberations that make the moon fall from the sky for want of orbits more celestially oblong and adjacent to the resonant heat that bears life a.k.a., music.

And you punk rock, art hermit holdouts, you think you are sticking it to the man by letting the man profit off the culture you built? You stick it to the man by owning that shit and making them come to you to use it. Fuck selling out, make 'em buy in.

Oh, did we ever talk merch?

QUICKLY ON MERCH

Merch, or artist merchandise, is the same printed product you see at your current job—only it's not your company logo emblazoned on a mug that sits in your garage collecting old bottlecaps and extra Ikea screws, it's the Oasis logo emblazoned mug that sits on your cubemate's desk that he air drums on with the pens he unsheathes from his other Oasis emblazoned mug that doubles as Oasis pen quiver.

"You're my wonderwah-ah-alll!"

Shirts, hats, hoodies, beanies, posters, stickers, coosies, bottle openers, snowbaords, marinara sauce, anything that can hold a print. Or, in the words of my Uncle Bepo "were talkin' high quality shit over here!"

The merch business is selling of such "quality shit."

Now the merch business is the quintessential complementary business. It is an additional monetization mechanism for an artist who has a defined customer base that is demanding more products. Customers, "fans," buy more shit they don't need but absolutely love and each purchase reinforces their passion for you and increases their repeat purchase potential. Win win win win.

(True, today merch is merging with fashion so there is an entirely new market for merch that is either: 1) made by an artist the buyer doesn't listen to, they just love the brand and/or 2) made strictly as a fashion brand. Yes, that's called a brand, we covered this already.)

Remember, you sell merch *because* people love your music, *because* you are a star, *because* they already bought your LP and want more stuff, *because* they love you and want anyone that will listen / look / walk into their bedroom to know they are a fan of you.

And, pay attention label execs, let's not leave out physical music. Half of merch today is aging music product—vinyl, cassettes, USB sticks, even CD's—fans already have the digital version of the music to listen to, this goes on the wall, the shelf, the coffee table. Said another way, it is not going to be opened, let alone listened to.

All that said this business is shit. I mean, it's a great complementary income stream if you have done the work of becoming a successful artist, I am talking about the nuts and bolts of operating the business. It's super hard work, super low margins, majority physical products that you have to put up cash for, in advance, then ship and carry around in bags and boxes and vans and post offices. Basically it's heavy stuff you need to make and sell. And nobody wants to do that. That's why we buy stuff online and have it shipped to us the same day.

And for those scoffing or holding on to the DIY myth, you know what the larger "merch" industry is called outside of music? The "consumer products industry," a.k.a., a multi trillion dollar global industry impacted by every indicator from commodity prices to if it snowed over a holiday weekend. Your manager, drummer, the buddy who made t-shirts in high school, are not gonna make a ripple in that ocean. This business is best left to the companies with the business model to make it a worthwhile enterprise; big cash, big distribution network, high product diversity, existing global accounts, world class sales force, massive economies of scale.

I am telling you it may feel like a lot of money selling twenty $20 shirts and a few vinyls every night until you have to pay for tees, printing, bags, labels, shipping, records, boxes, tables, signs, an extra guy on the road that ends up mostly smoking way too much and crashing the van.

Yeah, so let's not shall we? Let's leave this to the big guys with the reach and expertise to handle it. That is a professional organization that makes, ships and sells physical goods into retailers around the world. You, artist, just consider merch to be what it is. When there is demand for your music, there will be demand for your merch and when that hits, hire someone great to do it for you.

Oh, and in the meantime, make one style shirt in one colorway (hello my over 40 readers again, a "colorway" is a particular color combination on a product that is changed without changing the underlying product—think of Nike shoes, one style many "colorways") that has your band's name prominently displayed on it and only deal in cash. This will allow you to focus on the music and help kick start what one day might become a long term asset, your brand, or both. Meantime it'll help you get the three golden G's in your early touring days: grub,

164

gas, and grass.

Let a pro handle the merch and you worry about your music, your brand, your back.

QUICKLY ON MANAGERS

You have no idea how bad I want to write this chapter, but I can't. One of my main jobs is obviously being a manager and, based on the book thus far (don't worry its almost over), you get a sense that I am not the average breed. Thus I would describe the "proper" way to manage as my way of managing (otherwise why would I mange that way) and that is not only a conceited-ass stance, but totally biased and impractical. There are plenty of successful managers and artists navigating successful careers without me nor my tactics nor my philosophies.

So I will just say this, I know you trust the homie, but the homie is the homie for reason; mine too, that's why I put him in charge of ordering the whiskey at dive bars, betting horses at the track, and calling the Lyft when we've done too much of both, but not in charge of running my company.

You are entrusting your manager with your art, your livelihood; they will be your chief strategist, consoler, and confidant; the first one to know and the last one to leave. They are literally taking the stories from your soul and attempting to help provide 50+ years of your and your family's financial stability and prosperity. If they are not crazy humble, crazy smart, and your type of just plain crazy get one that is.

ARTISTS ARE NOT MADE THEY ARE DESTROYED

I have a friend, an artist, and I tell anyone working with him "don't ask what a song is about before 9a.m."

"Why?" They ask.

"Because he'll tell you."

Most people like to assume that their favorite artists depth and emotional tsunami is due to talent. It is not. It is due to stories rarely shared, cuz if they were, if you knew the personal price that great artists pay to create that three minute tune you just bobbed your head to on your lunch break, you wouldn't be able to finish whatever grease bomb the mustachioed gentledude just handed you out of the food truck window.

Back to work.

If you have the chance to go to music school, don't. In fact, if you want to be the greatest artist of all time, you should probably steer clear of all formal educational settings with the exception of perhaps primary school. I mean if you went to college you should likely just give up. Now, that's not to say you can't make a career in the music business or make a healthy living with a sustainable level of success as an artist, but the odds of setting fire to the world with your art are

166

nigh.

Why?

First, let's be clear that I am not here to crush dreams, in fact, I believe that the dreamers of the impossible are the backbone of society and the catalyst for all human progress—or to quote the late great Willy Wonka (who quoted the lesser known in pop circles Arthur O'Shaughnessy) "We are the music makers, we are the dreamers of dreams." And no artist can exist devoid of dreams, but that doesn't change the fact that formalized education is not exactly the platform for manifesting new eras of sound.

Why?

Art is born from suffering.

And great art is born from great suffering.

Although we tend to forget it given the modern discussions around music—copyrights, technology, piracy, celebrity, paparazzi, public meltdowns, premature declaration of death of this genre / that genre, content, brands, beef—but music is art. And art is the amalgamation personal experience and expression. The deeper of each the better the art. The further down the rabbit hole you go, the better the story when (if) you get back to the surface. Blues men on porches, the great women of jazz, psychedelic enhanced drifters, punk radicals, street corner rappers, these are not music theorists examining process, these are people with nowhere else to turn. This is life boiling over into audio.

We are not talking about the romantic tortured artist here. This is not the cute outcast just trying to fit in whom nobody understands is a genius. Sure that exists, the same way successful college of music graduate artists exist. I am talking about the enduring of and daily conquest over hardships and how that process forces you to retreat into self to find strength; how that struggle forces you to self analyze, self actualize and discover those hidden bits within you. The more isolated you are—physically, mentally, environmentally—the more into self you are forced to dive. And the further into self you dive, the deeper and richer the understanding of your own experience and thus the deeper and richer in all that you are creating around you. In your case, music.

And we often speak about an artist "finding their voice," well this is where its hiding.

Deep in the bowels of your being. Another of our simple, but not easy issues. First, no one is going to voluntarily look there. You may even believe my words as you read them, but its not going to make you do it. You can't. You can't just call up the latent. You can't take a class on mining subconscious thought. The only way to get there is to be forced. Your life circumstances coupled with genetic wiring puts you in a place that survival requires such a plunge. The more often you go, the longer you stay, the better the art. To a point. Stay too long and you're called crazy. Eccentric. Genius maybe.

Let me stop before I myself wind down a philosophical rabbit hole pontificating of the value of the deconstructed self in art. (Wtf does that even mean?)

The point of this chapter is simple, don't think of your depression, your anxiety, your pain, your isolation as hindrances—think of them as blessings, as secret weapons imparted to you so that you may make the world a more beautiful place, for all of us.

And for all of us, business types and fans, be sensitive to the human souls that make the music we love. A great price was paid.

But that price was not tuition, drop out now!

Sorry moms.

STREAM ME A SAVIOR

Stop. Just fucking stop. We wipe $20 billion off our revenue line due to an industry culture that celebrates five of the seven deadly sins (greed, gluttony, lust, pride, hubris for those keeping score) and some tech company puts a few back on the board by unbundling albums online and we are start throwing high fives? Talking about "if we can only open China now!" Good plan, let's once again follow a false prophet and put our fate in the hands of the industry that took us to destruction's front porch and look to a country that is, shall I say, the Sinatra of counterfeit physical goods to embrace digital legitimacy.

Yes, I know streaming will keep growing, yes, I know that means revenue will grow. And yes, I can do the math. The problem is the math is a tad more complex than: Planetary Population x Monthly Streaming fees = Future Recorded Music Income. And, as discussed, betting your industry on the assumption that there is inherent and inexhaustible value in our product because it had it in the recent past is negligent.

Or in the wise words of music legend Charlie Schwab—past performance is not an indicator of future returns.

But lets just say the recorded music revenues keep growing, that means we stop fucking innovating and trying to lead our business forward? We trade Jobs for Cook and our plan is to keep feasting off their table scraps because one facet of a dying business, i.e., records, feels a tad more secure based on adoption of a complementary technology?

These tech guys revolutionize an industry or three and go land homemade spaceships on Mars.

Mars.

So one of them figured out how to get all of our consumers on a tech platform that we don't own and send us penny fractions all while running run an unprofitable company and we are dancing in the streets?

Earth streets.

170

So what's an artist to do?

Collect your checks. You make enough noise in this business and the streaming services will send you some rent money, but don't rely on it. Make sure your label knows how to optimize your visibility on the services, make sure your PR team is reaching the people, make sure you are letting your fans know where to go to hear your art. Play the game for bit cuz this transition is gonna take some time and in the near term this is how people will consume your art. And there is money there I am not denying it, but it's not our future. Streaming even at 100 percent penetration still has some tech dude, a.k.a., not you, owning it and eventually looking to sell it to some investment company or struggling media conglomerate, neither of which gives two fucks about music, let alone artists. So get your money and use it to build your own rocket ship.

So what's our industry to do?

Start servicing artists and customers in a real way.

[Deleted*]

This section contained honest, vulgar, disparaging, accurate, trade secrets and fanciful speculation that included such insanity as treating artists like smart, capable human beings, forming strategic, reason-based, mutually beneficial partnerships with interdisciplinary industry stakeholders in an effort to push our art and industry into the future. In other words, music business nonsense. Thus, it was omitted by me on my second draft.

In 1860 the three-minute song was invented. These songs were bundled to make what we call "albums" one hundred years later. Fifty years after that, we unbundled them again threw them up on the Internet and called it the future of music. Sorry folks, streaming is a one hundred-fifty-year-old music format with a new delivery system and price.

Streaming is one of those pianos that plays itself.

Streaming is a less automated juke box.

Streaming is like a friend giving you a mixtape, except its not from your friend its from a robot who takes cash bribes.

I pay for streaming people, I am just not waiting for it to save my career.

I am waiting for some tween Danish hacker to release a machine learning bot that wirelessly plugs into the cloud and beams music into the iChip I surgically implant in my ear.

Onward.

THE END?

Not too long ago I had a corporate music executive wearing $500 out-of-fashion jeans drinking Perrier from his in-office wet bar tell me I was "smug."

This might be the perfect image of where we are as an industry. What they think is the latest thing is already out, when challenged with new ideas they condescend, and they just can't get rid of the wet-bar. I mean come on, a fucking wet-bar? And if you are gonna keep the bar you better own it and drink a midday scotch. Cuz the nostalgia they are clinging to wasn't a golden age, it was corporate malfeasance.

The danger is not the end of our industry its that our industry in refusing to end. If the fundamental model remains unchanged, we are doomed to repeat the past i.e. a short term cash jolt due to a updated delivery medium (streams) that will once again be upended by a new technology.

And its happening. As one exec recently described to me the money is "pouring back in". So we are pouring whiskey sodas, hold the whiskey as we arrive to work at 10 a.m. The same 10 a.m. the tech companies are restocking the electrolyte-enhanced-sea-algae-water bottles that were emptied after the voluntary four mile 6 a.m. corporate campus jog.

The same 10 a.m. tweens are fully satiated by the 42 pieces of non-audio-based media they are consuming on a 4 inch screen on the 3 minute walk from homeroom to 2nd period.

The same 10 a.m. teenager hackers are coming down from all-nighter Redbull buzzes as they pause on the code that will soon convert Spotify's music library into freely tradeable blockchain.

The same 10 a.m. college kids are starting AI companies that will forever relegate music to background noise in a simulated universe we will be able to access from our couches and Matrix-esque battery pods.

Ok, the last one goes too far, but the point is its all advancing, We humans are advancing and our tastes, our expectations, our entire experiential lives are undergoing such a rapid development that half the things we now "can't live without" didn't exist 5 years ago.

It's just math people, the "things we can't live without" are finite, music is not immune.

I was once asked, during my major label days, "Airaudi, what's the silver bullet?"

I responded, "One that splits into a million bullets."

At the time I meant simply that we needed stop looking for one big shot to kill one scary monster—file-sharing services, ISPs, broke kids who can code—and just needed to be ready to fight our way out of the trench before the onslaught arrived. No secret weapon, no master plan, just some close range combat coordinated by a bunch of folks that didn't feel like letting their industry die that day. Monsters weren't coming for us, progress was. But instead of embracing a culture of innovation, incubating varied new ideas, and seeking radical reinvention we chose to employ technologies that most closely resembled what we were accustomed to fighting with. So we were overrun.

We brought iTunes to a gun fight.

Truth is there is no bullet.

There are just artists in the eternal struggle to find value for creative work in an ever-changing marketplace ruled by standardization. There are just people who want auditory stimuli and those of us in a position to serve it. There is a business in flux, full of faults and fractures and triumphs and pity and humans and money. It's madness, but I love it. Music is the ultimate visceral connection. The music business is the ultimate riddle. They may make rockets to space, but imagine if that rocket woke up everyday and decided whether or not it wanted to launch.

That's our business, that's our journey.

And you, you are the captain.

So embrace your faults, embrace your demons, embrace your talents and your art. Embrace the power that has been bestowed to you to

make the world a bit better even if its bit by bit. Record by record. Show by show. Run this ship. Cuz I am for sure down to roll to Mars, as soon as you book your 1st gig there.

EPILOGUE

I woke up one morning in London to find a text on my phone with one of the most hurtful messages I have ever received. It told me I was a liar. A fraud. A hanger-on who "lusted" to be in the band. That I would never understand music nor artists. That I had done it all with a devilish calculation to destroy what they had built. Their money, their livelihood, their life. And that I would ultimately destroy them all.

And what as it that had I done?

Eight years earlier I had reached out to an interesting artist I admired online. For three years I had been their fan, then for five years I was their manager. I let them into my home. They literally stayed in my son's room while he voluntarily bunked up with his little brother. I cooked for and fed them at my table with my wife and daughters and sons and uncles and aunts and friends. I opened up all of my contacts and put my time, energy, money and reputation on the line to adamantly pitch them to everyone who would listen. I believed in them. I spent tens of thousands of dollars of my family's savings and years of my life to try to make their life dreams a reality.

And it didn't work.

And at the end of this road, after all of the ups and downs, laughs and tears, struggle and pain, all I got was a hurtful, personally disparaging note sent via text message.

And I deserved it. Not the personal disparagement, but fact is I failed to perform. I can say what I want about the music not "connecting" and songs not being "good enough" or my fucking condescending ass 3-Step Plan, but I made a promise to help them achieve success, I made them believe they had what it takes, that their dreams could be realized and I failed.

And that is this other side of the business.

Yes its product development, yes its efficient deployment of capital and execution of services, yes it's music, but more specifically it is the people and dreams business.

I have artists I have helped develop that have been successful and they are grateful for my professional guidance and friendship.

I have artists I have helped develop that have been successful and they do not even acknowledge I was part of the process.

I have artists I have helped develop that have been unsuccessful and are off trying their best on another path.

I have artists I have helped develop that have been unsuccessful and say it was 100 percent my fault.

They are all right.

In the music industry, we are monetizing dreams. We are creating a business where there was no intention of commercialization. We are taking art, pure emotive output in its rawest form and asking that it be the foundation of accolades, assets, income and longterm security. A "career" in music is an oxymoron. How do you build a career off an emotion? How do you create long term stability around something as fleeting as a feeling invoked via sound? Yet that is our attempt. Artist, executive, and entrepreneur.

People and dreams.

A noble pursuit, but be weary the task's weight. I tell my artists I am humbled by their belief in me, that I can be of service to them and aid in the achievement of the impossible—building a successful long-term career in music. And I am humbled. I don't sleep, I don't eat, I worry, I have been fetal position in the shower wondering how I am going to tell my wife we can't pay the rent and my band that no one cares about their album. (Entrepreneurial side note, if you have not experienced being crippled into fetal position in your shower by equal parts fear, anxiety, and guilt, you are not yet an entrepreneur—I say yet, because if you are and you haven't, it's coming!)

I don't say this because I want pity or a pat on the back, I say it because I want you to understand the heaviness of the music "business." This is the suffering you will adopt and carry if you chose to immerse yourself in the business of music. Notice I said immerse. You can get a job doing anything. I am not talking about jobs. I speak of obsession. If you are in this business and are not plagued by the burden of building dreams then you don't get it.

Music is making miracles with mortals.

For us, the business folks, we cannot forget that these artists are entrusting us with the whole of their being—both their emotive art, the output of the trials and triumphs of their lives at their most vulnerable state AND their ability to earn a living.

There is no way to overvalue that trust.

For the artist, you are entrusting your art and livelihood to human beings beset with all the standard human imperfections. Be mindful of the malicious ones, but there are very few of those, mostly be mindful that the people you entrust work *for* you not the other way around. You are the boss and while that sounds great, one thing all great bosses must be great at it is getting the best out of their people. The responsibility of success starts and ends with you.

There is no way to overvalue that responsibility.

If you are in the business of search algorithms and your search-page fails to load people are inconvenienced; if it works well peoples' lives are more convenient. If you make laptops and one breaks, someone needs to return it and get a new one; if it works well, they will likely purchase more of your products.

For our products however, it's a matter of peoples' lives. A persons' life's work and livelihood are behind each. If we fail, we fail the person. When we are successful, we can make positive change not only in that artist's life, but in the millions of listeners lives around the world.

I am not making a case to cheapen other industries, other work or people, I am just making a case for ours. Making the obvious statement that we in this business have a responsibility to stop pretending our industry is immune to business realities and stop blaming outside forces. There are no monsters, no villains, no heroes, no victors. There is just relentless change and unrelenting lovers of sound who think the world is better off with sound makers in it.

Here's to noble work.

Here's to people and dreams.

Here's to the music makers.

LUCK IS MADE. GODSPEED.

Printed in Great Britain
by Amazon